AMERICA
ISAIAH IS WARNING

GOD'S JUDGEMENT IS COMING

JOHN W MORGAN

Copyright © 2014 by John W Morgan

America, Isaiah is Warning: God's Judgment is Coming
by John W Morgan

Printed in the United States of America

ISBN 9781629524382

All rights reserved solely by the author. The author guarantees all contents are original and do not infringe upon the legal rights of any other person or work. No part of this book may be reproduced in any form without the permission of the author. The views expressed in this book are not necessarily those of the publisher.

Unless otherwise indicated, Bible quotations are taken from the New American Standard, 1995 Update Of The Bible. Copyright © 1995 By The Lockman Foundation.

www.xulonpress.com

This book is dedicated to two men, William Koenig and John P. McTernan, Ph.D., both of whom dedicated time, effort and treasure to make America's leaders and the American people alert to the messages sent from God, warning us of His impending judgment were we to continue our national deafness to His warnings. To step forward in defiance of mankind's wisdom and issue such bold statements against actions that most of the world gives, at least lip service of approval, invites ridicule and ostracism. Fully anticipating these twins of fools, they risked and endured both. Their warning went unheeded; yet, but for a few. For those of us, I take the opportunity to say thank you. You did not fail to call out; most to whom you called did not have ears to hear.

Contact John Morgan:

Website: www.fourth-watch.com

Email: john@fourth-watch.com

Mail: John Morgan

    Suite 100

    1712 Alameda Ct.

    Plano, TX 75074-3601

TABLE OF CONTENTS

Introduction xv

Chapter One: Storms 23

Chapter Two: Disasters 39

Chapter Three: The Unnamed Nation 64

Chapter Four: The Bad News 88

Chapter Five: The Narrow Way 131

Chapter Six: The Garden of the Secret Place 157

Chapter Seven: Spiritual Warfare and Summation 197

Appendix A: Isaiah 18 rendered in various translations 201

Appendix B: Christian foreshadowing in the Jewish wedding . . 209

End Notes 221

ACKNOWLEDGMENTS

This is the place to permanently imbed appreciation for the efforts of others who helped me. Writing a book takes a lot of effort and a lot of help. This is my first effort and the learning curve was sometimes steep. All of those whose names will follow can never fully appreciate how thankful I am for them, unless they trudge this same path.

> My wife Diane had to put up with many, "I can't do that now. I have to work on the book." She remained gracious and understanding throughout. I am just thankful I did not have to take 400 pages to get all of this written. I may have needed to add the word *usually* in the second sentence. In seriousness, after 50 years of marriage and six of those in stressful health on my part, I thank God daily that He smiled on me with His favor in this union.

- Since 2000, Glynda Lomax Linkous has been a friend indeed. Over these years we have been of mutual help to one another in our struggle for spiritual maturity. My appreciation here, however, is focused on her help with how to do this. She and husband Jerry are published co—authors, Christian radio show on Blog Talk Radio and select radio stations in the U.S. discussing prophecy. Having a resource of information to a new writer, as well as one starting an online ministry, her help has been invaluable. She has given her help graciously, consistently and encouragingly.

- Editing one's own writing of any length is a nearly impossible task. Good editors cost money and I did not have money to pay an editor. Not just anyone can be a good editor. More specifically, few qualify. Besides, it takes time and energy to read and correct someone else's writing. One of my cries for help went out through our high school Facebook page. God again showed favor. One of the smartest girls in our class volunteered to help me. Laverne Warner, Ph.D. is not only a smart, a lifelong friend of whom I am very proud, recently retired from the faculty of Sam Houston State University, in Huntsville, Texas and is now Professor Emerita. She is a Christian leader, a facilitator of help to others and very patient with an old friend who did not pay close enough attention in English class. I am blessed to have had so many in my high school class go on to achieve so much for themselves and others. They represented us well. Laverne is among the top tier.

- I brazenly asked some of my friends to spend their own time to read this manuscript for feedback as to content. To each of them I am so appreciative of their willingness to do so. Alphabetically, they are: James Adams, Scott Brady, Ann Harrington, Jack Level, Nick Shovlin and Carla Warnell. I treasure each one of you and I took to heart every comment you made.
- Catherine Pagoda Sanders, a dear friend and wife of Hershel, one of my high school's outstanding classmates. One of Catherine's many gifts is a wonderful sense of being able to graphically communicate essential concepts of the written word.

INTRODUCTION

Future events seem to fascinate the human mind. They certainly have mine. When I became serious about my Christian faith, I became fascinated that the Bible spoke directly about the future. Details were mystical to me, so I sought out explanations from so-called experts. My searches led me to a then best seller, *The Late Great Planet Earth* by Hal Lindsey. I read the book, saw the movie version and enthusiastically discussed the subject of the end times If any book were on the topic, it had my attention.

My study was not only about eschatology, this mystical study of the end times, but other scriptures in the Bible as well. After a time, not too long as I remember, I became less and less fascinated in those future days. I was drawing closer to God and Him to me. Eschatology diminished in importance for me as I had way too many other subjects to learn. Maybe you traveled much the same path in your early Christian walk. Perhaps, you are a new Christian and you are at that place now; the last days as some call the days of eschatology.

The difference between then, forty years ago, and now is the events of these days. In the days of Mr. Lindsey's *The Late Great Planet Earth* we were in a period of time which I would call an early awakening. One could barely make out the distant storm clouds of tribulation. As the saying goes, times have changed and I have changed, too. These last very few years, God has begun to deal with me again concerning the last days. He has made it perfectly clear to me and a host of other believers that we are walking through the door, if you will, of the time of Second Coming of Jesus Christ and what that entails for the world.

Quite frankly, I thought God had passed me over for some type of public ministry. We all think, at one time or another in our walk with Him, that He has us singled out for some ministry of really notable service. I came to grips with the reality, that for me, that was not to be. My ministry was to express His love for my brothers and sisters in the Lord and to share the good news about Jesus with whomever I could. I was okay with that role and contented to serve God in that way. Now that has changed.

Since I am not an author one would recognize, nor scholar with a list of credentials, why would one buy this genre from an

Introduction

unknown? Before I attempt to answer, let me pose another question, please. Does God speak to you? Is there a still small voice in your chest, or words you are saying which explain something biblically which you are hearing for the first time. Perhaps is it that peace of assurance or a troubled spirit within that you just know God is either affirming or warning you off. The answer to my first question as to why you should heed anything I say is best given by telling you how it came about. In 2002, I was reading the Book of Isaiah. As I finished the last verse, the familiar nuance nudged, go back to the first verse. Where are the rivers of Cush? What nation is beyond them? Thus preceded the revelation of what Isaiah is telling us. When super Storm Sandy pounded the Northeast I understood the cycle of warning was over. Repentance had not come, so judgment would have to follow. Some months later, God began showing me in various ways that I was to write this book; there were flash visions of the book in stores, books suddenly seemed to invade my life, I had an impelling need to communicate this story. Obediently and nervously, I began to write.

The subject of this book is out of the box, if you will. Most books that I have read on prophecy tell what is going to happen, as the author sees it. This one tells what just happened and what I see happening next. It is in real time, so to speak. Isaiah spoke these words 2,500 years ago, but only until 2012 did what he was saying become clear. He intimates diplomatic activity is what causes God's judgment to fall on the unnamed nation. We can now know who the nation is, what the diplomatic activity is, why God is impelled to judge. How He is going to do it and what year it will come are the only two unknowns, even so He is giving high probabilities. This much is for sure; the generation to hear and understand the prophecy of judgment will experience it.

The book can be split into three sections. The first is historical and is well documented with End Notes. The final section is practical, biblical applications for surviving in the aftermath of the judgment. It is the middle section where the seven verses are dissected. We will look at them through the exegetical process of study. I trust it will be thorough enough.

My ministry now is to be that of a watchman on the wall. A quick history lesson may be in order to put what this means in focus for our time. In biblical times, cities were walled for protection. Protection for the citizens was provided by watchmen who were appointed a shift of a few hours each to man a portion of the city's walls. The Jews had four numbered watches between dusk and dawn, the fourth being the last, as you might expect. The fourth watch was the most critical because then, as now, ground armies

Introduction

like to begin attacks just before dawn. Spiritually, I believe we are in the fourth watch, on alert for what Jesus warned would be a great tribulation. That is why the address for my website for this ministry is www.fourth-watch.com.

A watchman has no special talents. God has put in place an outer perimeter warning system, if you will. It consists of Bible prophecies, the sun, moon followed by celestial bodies. The Holy Spirit awakens the watchman to an event to which one of the above point in order for him to give the shout of warning. His responsibility is to be alert and shout the warning. This is not prophecy. God is not speaking something He has not already said, so watchmen do not say, "Thus saith the Lord..." It works more like this; the Bible predicts an event. As the event is about to occur, confirming activity witnesses its arrival. The Spirit of God reveals the coming fulfillment to the watchman. That is exactly what this book is about: the coming fulfillment of prophecy.

Prophecy is not fulfilled in a vacuum. Events proceed and follow its fulfillment. We are going to cover those preceding events. When we finish, we will discuss the prophecy and then attempt to look into the aftermath based on biblical insights. Along the way there may be some Rabbit Trails. A Rabbit Trail in this writing is somewhat like an aside is in a theatrical production where an actor turns to the audience during the performance and gives them a bit of useful information. I hope Rabbit Trails will edify your knowledge base should you not already be aware of the information. So, there are three main sections: the history of events which make the prophecy understandable in time, the prophecy itself and suggestions on the best way to live during the fulfillment and aftermath.

There are four takeaways I wish to emphasis here. They are dealt with in detail in the text, of course. As you read, my prayer is that I have communicated clearly what God wanted me to tell you. Here are the takeaways:

First, the mathematical probability of the events in the chapter entitled *Storms* just being that of a series of coincidences is off the charts. It is impossible each of these happened randomly. Ergo, something or someone caused them. The challenge then becomes to answer the questions who and why?

Second, the scripture in which I received revelation that the unnamed nation was indeed the United States of America has two major components of identification. The first is geographical. The prophecy uses geographical pointers to the nation. These can be found on any world globe. When the direction to which they point is followed, there are a finite number of nations to which it could be referring. Only one will have the major topographic features. The other component is the description of the people, how they are viewed from an international viewpoint and a specific activity, which is the catalyst for the resulting judgment.

Third, is to come to understand the significance of a covenant. And, congruently, that covenant actions supersede all other actions.

Fourth, is the full comprehension of the words abide and dwell when the Bible uses them in the sense of the spirit. Of all the four, this one is the most important. Acceptance and knowledge of the other three pale in comparison this point. If a person does not understand this, it cannot be implemented in his life. If not a part of his life, then within the next few months, or at most the next few years, he will begin living as though he were in a horror movie.

Rabbit Trail #1

As you read through the book you will occasionally find the words *Rabbit Trail* in bold type, just like the one above. They are consecutively numbered within each chapter only for your reference.

And now, our first Rabbit Trail: a practical application of Philippians 4: 6, 7: Be anxious for nothing, but in everything by prayer and supplication with thanksgiving let your requests be made known to God. And the peace of God, which surpasses all comprehension, will guard your hearts and your minds in Christ Jesus. I encourage you to ask God before you start Chapter One, and every time you resume reading, to give you peace when these written words are true and to disturb you when they are not. I also recommend you ask the Holy Spirit to make you aware of this discomfort. Presence of the peace of God is a state of calmness in your spirit and mind. One may be intently interested, but not feeling at all ill at ease. When peace is not present a person senses a state of being uncertain or unsure. With me it is sometimes feeling uncomfortable without being sure why. Every time I began to write, I asked the Holy Spirit to give me the words to type. I have God's peace that He did just that. When He did not answer a specific question, I tell you, so that you are clear it is coming from my natural understanding, not through my spirit.

Enough of being on a Rabbit Trail, let's get started.

CHAPTER ONE: STORMS

*One incident is random, two are a coincidence
and three make a pattern*

Off New England's Coast in late October, 1991

The next wave collided with the bow more quickly than the one before and in its haste to arrive it germinates the seed of doubt. Doubt then began its invasion of the Captain's consciousness. Fear overtook and replaced doubt. Doubt and then came fear. Was this current weather going to hold? If so, his lobster trawler, *She Can Do It*, could easily handle these seas. Experience told him it would not hold. The doubt and fear were over the rate of change in this rapidly worsening sea. He stole a glance at his First Mate standing with him in the pilothouse. After so many years together, words were not necessary. The captain knew that doubt and fear were not unique to him that day. The expression on his trusted companion's face spoke loud enough. The First Mate then observed that the horses' tails were beginning to disappear, not a good sign as they had only been present for several minutes. Horses' tails is the nautical term for foam being blown off the tops of waves in a Gale Force wind. As the wind increases the foam doesn't form. Deepening swells could only mean an increasing wind. The ocean off the New England coast often turned mean when a fall weather front passed. Through the rain-battered windshield both men saw the swells were definitely deepening. This storm was worsening at an alarming rate.

The two men looked at each other, eyes locked. The years of being together in other perilous situations required no words to convey the inner thoughts. Each knew. Only madness would suggest running lobster pots today. A worse state of madness was to have stayed when the weather began to worsen with a radio having a short. As though a command had been spoken, the First Mate hit the side of the radio hard with the palm of his hand. He hit it once again. "Nothing", was his complete diagnosis. "What was the definition of idiocy?" thought the Captain. "Oh yes, repeating the same thing expecting different results."

He gave in. It had only been two minutes since he noticed the speed of the waves increasing. No matter how badly they needed revenue from a catch, he couldn't risk this. He turned the wheel and she began the slow arc to reverse direction. As she came abeam of

Chapter One: Storms

the waves, she rolled to and fro in the heavy seas. Waves washed over the gunnel and onto the deck as she broadsided the waves; props fighting against the will and strength of the water. Both men struggled to maintain their balance. She came around finally. The stern was now running with the waves. Things should be smoother now. Tension in the cabin eased a bit. Thirty minutes passed and the weather held. Then, and very suddenly, it worsened.

At first, he thought his eyes were deceiving him, but no. The swells were now in front of him again. They were also growing fast. The last one was nearly sixty feet tall. Fear returned with ferocity. As he fought the wheel to maintain his heading back to the New England coastline, his mind raced back through his catalogue of experience to explain the change in direction of the swells. "To be out here with a gimpy radio was madness," he berated himself. "Staying after the weather began to worsen was sheer madness." Sanity aside, their only job now was to return to a safe harbor. Plenty of time then for chastisement once they were tied up. Headway was decreasing and she rolled dangerously from port to starboard. Rising over each swell became more difficult; the ride down more perilous. The risk was very high that on these downward plunges the bow would drive into the sea so deeply the props would not have the strength to pull her through and recover. She would continue her underwater plunge toward the bottom.

Water was over the deck now, coming from every direction it seemed. In a moment of frozen amazement, he focused on the next on coming wave. In an instant, he knew his life was over. He, his trusted companion of all these years, and the two crewmen below deck, along with his beloved trawler, were all going to be dead within one minute. This coming wave must be 100 feet tall. He had never witnessed one nearly as tall. It was like it was out of a nightmare, but it was very much real and the harbinger of death itself. There was nothing he could do. In those last moments, the explanation for this weather's behavior became clear: they were going to die in a perfect storm, the convergence of three weather systems. Their climb up the towering swell began. It never finished. The last conscious moments of awareness were no longer of doubt or fear. Rather, sheer terror. Terror and, over the din of the raging sea, he was also vaguely aware of the words in his ear. "It was a good run, Cap 'in."

The Present

Our doomed Captain's experience in the storm is analogous to the near past and imminent future of the United States of America. The Ship of State, represented by his trawler, was also caught unawares in a sudden, perfect storm. Escape would only be possible by seeking

Chapter One: Storms

safe harbor early, as it was for *She Can Do It*. In the nation's case, safe harbor would be a change of national policy. However, just as he found out when the fronts converged and spelled his doom, so also is the convergence of the systems of our perfect storm: covenant, myopic national self-interest and the absence of spiritual leadership to connect the warning message's dots by not having ears to hear or eyes to see.

What follows can be broken into three sections. The first, what immediately follows is recent history. We begin with October, 1991 and end with October, 2012. However, the historic pattern continues and, in all probability it will continue for a time. What follows this pattern is in the second section. Events in section one predicate section two, which is the fulfillment of a 2,500 year old prophecy. And, yes, it is in the Bible. The initial outcome of the prophecy will change America forever and the rest of the world, as well. For those who are alive when it comes to pass should find the third section most helpful. It offers practical suggestions on how anyone can best survive what the prophecy portends.

In the Introduction, I talked about some other important considerations toward understanding what you will read. If you have not read the Introduction, I urge you to mark your spot and break off to read it.

October 30, 1991

As our captain noticed the changing sea, far to the east, another weather front had crossed the British Isles before entering the Bay of Biscayne along the northern Spanish Coast. The beautiful coastal resort city of Gijon was experiencing unusually strong winds and much colder temperatures than the average 62° Fahrenheit for the end of October. Inland, in the capital of Madrid, the weather would remain normal for this time of the year. Far enough away to not be disturbed by the storm to their north, they were, as well, oblivious to the storm across the Atlantic. Weather conditions were was immaterial to those attending the conference which was being held in the Royal Palace. And what a shame those conditions were immaterial, because had they connected the storm for what it was, a warning that their impending actions would serve to cause a diplomatic storm which would end up engulfing the whole world. They did not so the United States proceeded to step on to the world's stage to propose what the administration believed, in all their human wisdom, to be best for the Middle East and for the United States.

When did it begin? How far back does one have to go in order to see when the tentacles of this conflagration began to grab the United States and pull her presidents into their grasp of the Middle East? One might think the fuel for this fire was kindled by the shuttle diplomacy

Chapter One: Storms

of Henry Kissinger during the Nixon administration. That thought only begs the question; why did Nixon send Kissinger? No, it was earlier. It was when the United Nations granted statehood to Israel. On May 14, 1948, Israel became a nation and fulfilled the centuries old prophecy from Isaiah 66:8; who has heard such a thing? Who has seen such things? Can a land [nation] be born in one day?

Within months, war erupted between some of her Arab nations and the new fledgling state. Israel won, but the wars would continue intermittently until they totaled six. Yet to be fulfilled are two more. The last will be the infamous Battle of Armageddon. Wars and their rumors are symptomatic of this troubled region that has reached across the Atlantic and, with her tentacles of chaos, has drawn the United States into her web. We know this because now, in Madrid, Spain on October 30, 1991, we have the President of the United States publically stepping into the Middle East Conflict. In so doing, future administrations would follow for the same misguided

> *For you have heard that it was said, "THOU SHALL NOT COMMIT ADULTERY"; but I say to you that everyone who looks at a woman with lust for her has already committed adultery with her in his heart.*
> Matthew 5: 27, 28
>
> **Men are condemned by intent. Nations, governed by men, bring God's condemnation the same way through intent of the nation's leaders.**

reasons. It was not out of malice. It was out of spiritual blindness to words in the Bible. The country was now committed. No longer are representatives shuttling back and forth between Israel and her Arab neighbors seeking an accommodation allowing peace to break out between them. Now, the United States of America was marshaling a coalition of man's wisdom in the form of other nations to forge peace. A peace, were it to come to pass, that would make a liar of God.

The most powerful man on earth and the second most powerful man have met to meet with representatives of other nations whom they have invited to sit down and discuss how to reach peace in the region. George H. W. Bush opens the conference in the Royal Palace in Madrid. He will be followed by his co-sponsor, Mikhail Gorbachev, President of the Soviet Union. Those gathered to hear them are international representatives of nations of the world. The purpose: establish a framework for peace in the region. This framework will quickly morph into what will become known as land for peace.

Across the Atlantic, a storm had formed off the coast of Nova Scotia. Instead of following the normal weather pattern of west to east, it reversed and began a return trek west for the United States northeastern coast, a little over 1,000 miles away. In the ocean, just off the New England coast, it collided with a front moving east,

Chapter One: Storms

just leaving the shoreline in a normal weather pattern. As they met, they were saturated with tropical moisture from dying Hurricane Grace. The result was a storm at sea of one hundred foot waves, as witnessed by our fictional dead captain. Its large size reached back to the US coast and battered Maine with thirty foot waves. During a news interview a weather forecaster mentioned this confluence of weather patterns forming the perfect storm. Thus, the media had a name: The Perfect Storm.

As the storm spent its fury against the Maine coast, it did heavy damage to one particular property at Kennebunkport, that of President George H. W. Bush.

Rabbit Trail #1

I didn't bring up how the Perfect Storm formed for a lesson in meteorology. I bring it up because I want to share something with you of which you may not be aware. There is significance in the fact it was a storm formed by three confluences of weather. It is on the number three I want to focus. In Genesis One, the third day of creation was the day God made the waters over the earth recede to reveal the dry land. From that point on, the number three has been used by God as a way to show something is hidden and if you will look closely, He will reveal it to you. It is another way in which He communicates with us. One example is from the Second Chapter in

John's gospel. The wedding in Cana is on the third day. It is during this wedding that Jesus turns the water into wine, but that isn't the hidden message God is revealing. It is the fact that *Jesus* is the long awaited Messiah. I just thought you might find this interesting if you didn't already know it. Now, we need to go back to October, 1991.

The Perfect Storm gained a place in the memory of Americans alive at the time. It became part of our lexicon. It even has a book [1] and movie [2], both entitled The Perfect Storm.

August 26, 2001

We are going to jump to the date on history's timeline of August 26, 2001. It is now ten years after the Madrid Conference and the Perfect Storm. On this day, Saudi Arabia's Ambassador, Prince Bandar, is invited into the Oval Office to meet with the President of the United States. Joining President George W. Bush, son of the former President Bush, is the United States Secretary of State, Collin Powell. The usual affable Prince is particularly somber and serious as they sit down. It is obvious he has something of a grave nature to discuss with America's leaders. He quickly gets to the point. He has a message to deliver directly to the President from the Saudi Crown Prince, leader of Saudi Arabia. Prince Bandar opens his briefcase and takes out one page. He begins to read the Crown Prince's words. The Crown Prince notes the recent suicide bombings by Palestinians

Chapter One: Storms

in Israel have resulted in Israeli retaliation. In the Crown Prince's view, the retaliation has killed or injured a far greater number of Arabs than the suicide bombers caused in Israel. The Crown Prince concludes that the United States has made a strategic decision to support Israel's taking thousands of Palestinians' lives for, as the Crown Prince sees it, just a drop of Jewish blood. Prince Bandar goes on to read, "...the Crown Prince will not communicate in any form, type or shape with you, and Saudi Arabia will take all its political, economic and security decisions based on how it sees its own interest in the region without taking into account American interests anymore." [3]

The Ambassador leaves amid a mix of subtle pleasantries of goodbyes. When the door closes, the President and Secretary of State look at each other with stunned expressions, bordering on shock. What they both understood from the Crown Princes' message was this: America, you can forget about the free flow of oil at market prices and whatever cooperation you get from us in the future will be because it totally benefits us.

The best analogy to what this meant to America is this; if the blood supplies life to the body, then, oil supplies health to the economy. Almost any product in America depends on oil in one way or the other. Without stable oil prices or worse, the dependable availability of oil, the economy of the United States would crumble in shambles. These two men grasped the implications and sat down to consider a response, a quick response. It was ready in two days.

August 28, 2001

The letter the President drafted for the Crown Prince of Saudi Arabia was dated August 28, 2001. Within the two pages was one section which was history making. President Bush wrote, in part, that the United States had not changed its strategic position. The President goes on, "I firmly believe the Palestinian people have a right to live… in their own state…just as the Israelis…their own state." No president had ever made such a strong statement and in doing so, proclaims Israel to be occupying, in part, Arab homeland, not the covenant land given by God. This unprecedented statement in our Middle East involvement was akin to starting a turn while driving a car. Once executed, the car could never return to the exact, same vector it had been on. Likewise, our policy had just taken a turn…away from Israel. We would not be able to return. We will see a bit later why this was so egregious to God.

August 30, 2001

Two days later, His Majesty calls the President. It is August 30, 2001. After pleasantries,

Chapter One: Storms

The Crown Prince gets to the subject of the United States' new position. He stresses the importance of a public declaration to "... eliminate the common impression prevailing in the region of the U.S. bias toward Israel." The President promised to do so in two weeks, the week of September Tenth. [3] The turn of US policy has been completed.

August 30, 2001 fell on a Thursday. Days passed and the Week of the Tenth came for the President's promised public announcement. It would be drowned out in the deluge of other events, but what was agreed to was agreed to and what was said was said. Who heard did not matter.

September 11, 2001

Tuesday, two weeks from the day he had made the promise; the weather across America was beautiful. Early that morning, the President had left Washington for Florida to help promote some pending education legislation. However, Air Force One was not the only plane in the skies that clear Tuesday morning of September 11, 2001.

Anyone in the world with access to a television was able to be a proxy witness to the attack.

The carnage ensuing before us on our televisions or over our radios was testimony enough for every American to understand a major change in our world was taking place before our eyes. Four civilian passenger airliners became missiles under the control of Islamic terrorists. All four would have been successful were it not for brave Americans on Flight 93, who were willing to give their lives to protect others. The lives lost, the broken hearts, the heroic acts, the staggering costs are so seared into our memories, and there is no need to recount them here. The question of why God allowed this to happen confronted many Christian Americans.

June 24, 2002

President Bush, in a speech, formally calls for the establishment of a Palestinian state to live side by side Israel in peace, along with other principles that would become the framework for the Roadmap for Peace.

June 30 to July 6, 2002

Extreme rains the last five days of June produce flooding in the Hill Country and South Central Texas. The area is near President Bush's Texas ranch.

April 30, 2003

Coming out of the failed Oslo Accords between Israel and the Palestinians, the Quartet (USA, Russia, the European Union and the United Nations) develops the Roadmap for Peace. On this date, the plan is formally announced. It was never implemented.

May 3, 2003

In New Hampshire, a granite outcropping over 1,500 years old breaks off and collapses. The outcropping suggested the profile of a man and became popularly known as the Old Man of the Mountain. Daniel Webster, noted prosecutor in the famous Scopes trial, orator, author, politician and one time nominee for President gave the outcropping notoriety when he wrote, "Men hang out their signs indicative of their respective trades; shoe makers hang out a gigantic shoe; jewelers a monster watch, and the dentist hangs out a gold tooth; but up in the Mountains of New Hampshire, God Almighty has hung out a sign to show that there He makes men." It received other claims to fame.

I don't point this out as a disaster, rather to merely show God speaks to us in many ways, just as the Book of Hebrews attests. To me, God is saying that the kind of man who was of the formation of America is no more. I do not mean this as slam against President Bush. He is a man of his time who is not the same kind of man whose ideas formed this nation. America has crossed the proverbial Rubicon.

Rabbit Trail #2

Rabbi Jonathan Cahn answers the question of why in his New York Times best-selling book, *The Harbinger: The Ancient Mystery that Holds the Secret of America's Future*.[4] Though set in the genre of a novel, the facts of the story are true. While a very compelling read, a movie on DVD by WND is, in my opinion, better for the serious student of the Bible. Its title is *The Isaiah 9:10 Judgment: Is There an Ancient Mystery that Foretells America's Future.* [5] Rabbi Cahn's thesis is that 9/11 was a replication of what God permitted to happen to Israel by the Assyrians during the Seventh Century, B. C. and for the same purpose. It was a breech in Israel's and the United States' defenses to show our powerlessness without God's protection and the response of arrogance on the part of both nations. His argument is compelling. He has detractors who, again in my opinion, are spiritually blind. The evidence Rabbi Cahn presents is over whelming and totally consistent with God in action.

For our purpose, the message is that God was warning our country we were moving in a direction leading to grave danger. To borrow a Navy phrase, the 9/11 attack was only a shot across the bow of what would befall us were we to stay on the same course. We all share the responsibility; it is our leaders who man the tiller. (I can't stay away from Navy analogies. Well, after all, it is the Ship of State.) Our leaders were spiritually blind to the message, as their predecessors had been since 1991.

CHAPTER TWO: DISASTERS

A cycle completes when it returns from whence it started

2004

The Perfect Storm, the Madrid Conference and the damage to Bush's personal property at Kennebunkport causes two men, John McTernan and Bill Koenig, to begin to connect natural disasters in America with the government's active role in squeezing Israel on the land for peace issue. Over the next few years it becomes obvious to the two the events were not coincidences. Each major event, which was very bad for one part of America, made it a lead story nationally. Each was closely connected in time with the United States putting pressure on Israel to give up some of her land for a Palestinian state in exchange for neighboring Arab countries not waging war on Israel. The pattern of these two events occurring nearly simultaneously in time could not be random; someone had to be orchestrating them. It must be a message with a single theme.

They co-author a book entitled *Israel: The Blessing or the Curse*.[6] Through it, God made perfectly clear His messages of warning. The book was delivered to the White House and every member of Congress.

2008

In 2006 and again in 2008 the book, *Eye To Eye: Facing the Consequences of Dividing Israel*,[7] is updated under the same title by Bill Koenig. It is still available. It documents the following events under the administrations of Bush, Clinton and Bush. The thread which connects all of the disasters is that they occur within seven days of the United States squeezing Israel to relinquish land God had given them through a covenant He had made with Abram (later God changed Abram [exalted father] to Abraham [father of a multitude]):

- Nine of the ten costliest insurance events in U.S. history
- Six of the seven costliest hurricanes in U.S. history
- Three of the four largest tornado outbreaks in U.S. history
- Nine of the top ten natural disasters in U.S. history ranked by FEMA relief costs
- The two largest terrorism events in U.S. history

John McTernan authored a compelling sequel to *Israel: The Blessing or the Curse* in 2006 entitled *As America Has Done to Israel*.

[8] In it, he traces the history of the Jewish people and how the United States is unique among nations through blessing the Jews. With great detail he reveals the connection between America interfering with God's prophetic plan for Israel and awesome disasters striking America. Mr. McTernan continues his online ministry concerning the end times. Bill Koenig is now a White House correspondent and president of Koenig's International News, an online news source and commentary. Both men continue to sound the alarm as a watchman on the wall.

As George W. Bush changed the paradigm with his pledge to honor a Palestinian state on

Israeli land, the paradigm is going to change again under the Presidency of Barack Obama. This time it will be a sea change. Before we go back to his inauguration, I want to be certain of your understanding of the power of covenant relationship. This is, perhaps, the longest Rabbit Trail we shall take.

Rabbit Trail #1

There is nothing in our culture which duplicates the covenant of the Old Testament (OT). Between individuals, the closest thing would be a contract. It is the closest thing, but it is not very close. Between nations, it would be a treaty. In the years of ancient history, treaties were ratified by covenants between most nations. But treaties of today lack many of the essential elements. So then, what is a covenant?

This is a quote from the Anchor Bible Dictionary. Since this part is kind of like school and research, I urge you not to zone out while reading this.

> *By their very nature, covenants are complex enactments. As complex acts they combine: (1) historical events that create relationships, usually (though not necessarily) between unequal partners; (2) customary ways of thinking characteristic of both parties, especially common religious ideas associated with deities; (3) descriptions of norms for future behavior (which are often confused with "laws"); (4) literary or oral forms in which the agreement is couched; and (5) almost always some ritual act that is regarded as essential to the ratification of the binding promise. It follows that a covenant cannot be understood merely by regarding it as a rigid literary form, nor can it be understood by reducing it to a literary law code, a ritual act, or a theological or political idea or concept. Thus, most studies of*

Chapter Two: Disasters

OT covenant in the past quarter century that have been delimited by one or another of such concepts have largely generated a great deal of unnecessary confusion. [9]

Covenants are usually between a stronger and a weaker party. It was binding by death. Usually, an animal was sacrificed as part of the ritual. It drove home to the vassal in the covenant the penalty to himself and his family should he break the covenant. To the stronger party who broke the covenant, a curse would come which would destroy his kingdom. This ritual ratified the covenant.

While we are on breaking the covenant, let me distinguish between breaking and violating. Violations resulted in discipline. Breaking resulted in death. An example of violating is the grumbling during the exodus from Egypt. Going to Sinai, the people grumbled about their condition, water and food. God did nothing. On their way from Sinai they continued to grumble and God disciplined them. Leaving Sinai they were in covenant and only violated it with an attitude of distrust expressed in their complaining.

Why is understanding the covenant so important? We will answer that shortly. Then, in a later chapter we will come back to the most important covenant one can have in this life. We will see why, in the future, being a part of this covenant may well unlock the key to one's life or one's death.

Now we come to the Abrahamic covenant. It is the reason for the near death blow to the United States. So let us go back in time and refresh our memory about this man called Abram from the Ur of the Chaldees. The Chaldees was in the southern part of today's Iraq. Politically, it was a part of Shinar, Nimrod's kingdom and the home of infamous Babel. Shinar would become Babylon. Ur was, of course, a city in the Chaldees where Abram's father Terah lived, along with Abram and his other sons Nahor and Haran. The account begins in Genesis 11. Archeological records show Ur was a center of sin. In Joshua 24:2, we are told both Terah and Haran were both idol worshippers. The Genesis account tells us that Haran died in Ur in front of his father, Terah. Most likely it indicates Terah was the cause of Haran's death which may have occurred during the ritual worship of a false god.

For some reason, the Bible doesn't say why, Terah decided to move to Canaan. Perhaps, it had to do with Haran's death. Nevertheless, their first major stop was the city of Haran. Again, the Bible does not tell us why, but it does say that Terah died there in Genesis 11:32. Then God spoke to Abram and told him to continue to the land He would show him. Abram obeyed the voice of God and took his wife Sari, his nephew Lot (son of Haran) and his servants and left, leaving his brother Nahor and his family behind in Haran. Haran is again a place of destination in the Bible. It is the place Jacob is told to go to escape Esau's rage toward him for stealing his blessing. The reason Jacob went to Haran is because his uncle, Latham, son of Nahor, lived there. When God spoke to Abram, He not only told him to leave Haran and go to the land He would show him, He also said some other remarkable things.

Connected to the obedience of going was the promise from God of making Abram a great nation and through him all the other nations of the world were to be blessed. He was going to do this for Abram while blessing him. So Abram knew he was to have something his imagination could not grasp, but it was going to be good, because God also promised something else. He promised to bless (cause positive increase) to those who brought positive increase to Abram. To those who did the opposite of blessing him and treated Abram with disregard for who he was, showing him contempt, God would remove the blessing of increase, meaning destruction would befall that person. The actual verse reads: And I will bless those who bless you, and the one who curses you I will curse. [10] In the paraphrase of this verse, which I gave you first, the meaning of the two different Hebrew words translated *curse* are given. All of these words will later be formally ratified by a covenant God makes with Abram. Once the covenant is ratified by the blood of the two of them (God being represented by a burning fire pot) between the split heifer and other sacrifices, it is in force and tied to Abram. The promises of the covenant and Abram are one in God's eyes and because God has not died, the covenant is still in force between Himself and Abraham's descendants, because God ratified the covenant first with Isaac and then, again, with Jacob!

Reflect on what you have read so far about the disasters connected to pressuring Israel. Now, add to that knowledge the understanding of the covenant concerning the land. God gave it to Abram, who became Abraham, then reaffirmed it to his son Isaac, then reaffirmed it again to his son Jacob. The covenant passed down through this line from Abraham. It continues to the Jews of today. Israel is their land. Remember the curse: I will curse those who curse you. Again, there are two different Hebrew words used for our word translated *curse*. The first means to treat lightly, to treat with contempt, to ignore. The second means to banish, to remove from the blessing. The point is simple. Whoever treats Abram and the covenant with contempt (not worth heeding) God will banish from the blessing. Since God is binding himself to Abram through the covenant, this would then be obligatory and read: but the one who treats you with contempt I must curse.

We have read about several people and the names can become confusing. They are not as nearly confusing as genealogical records.

If you have ever been on a bible reading plan and come to a seemingly endless list of names, which few you know and even more you can't pronounce and will probably never read about again, you have to wonder why God put all that in there. I don't begin to question God's purpose for genealogical records, but it is a fair question to ask. There are at least four reasons I can give which answer part of His reason.

First, the Bible is a historical record. In that record are real people. Their genealogy is important for us to understand who was on the stage of biblical history at any given time. It also establishes the record through whom the Seed of Promise passed and where it stopped in man and then began again in the spirit of man in the form of a rebirth, or a man being born again. And note this, with every rebirth in the spiritual genealogy the person is always the generation of the First Fruit. We are all born of the same Spirit.

Second, some records include a timeline of the father's lifespan and his age at the birth of his first born son, who will most certainly be next in the record. This enables us to know their place in history and number of generations.

Third, Hebrew names have meanings. They can be a clue to understanding that part of the text, but not always. Don't treat it as a rule, but here is one example. The following is the lineage of Abram from Noah. The meaning follows in italics. These can be found in any good concordance. In parenthesis, I have my explanation of the meaning.

Noah = *rest* (don't strive to be your own god, doing life your way)

Shem = *name* (the summation of who a person is)

Arpachshad = *I shall fail as the breast, he cursed the breast-bottle* (he cursed that which part of himself that was to give the food of life)

Shelah = *sprout* (a new beginning)

Eber = *the region beyond* (a different environment and place to grow)

Peleg = *division* (complete separation)

Reu = *friend* (one trustworthy, dependable)

Serug = *branch* (from a spout, to a trunk, off a trunk to be able to produce fruit)

Chapter Two: Disasters

Nahor = *snorting* (connected with God's anger in the Bible, but not His wrath)

Terah = *station* (place one is supposed to be)

Abram = *exalted father* (one whose station is elevated above others through the children he sires)

What I understand this to say is that the new beginning with Noah was for man to stop being his own god. The man turned out to be the opposite. So, God cursed that nature in man. He began another new beginning for man and gave him a different place than the physical realm in which to grow, separated from the contamination of the god/man nature — a nature with which He could be the trustworthy, dependable friend. That sprout of man was to grow to the point man would be able to reproduce the nature of God in the physical realm. Deviation from this kind of growth would produce God's anger. However, as long as man stayed in the place of growth God provided, then he would be exalted above those who did not and his fruit would have within it seeds of its own for new life. You see it? It is a prophecy of what Abram was to produce: man in relationship with God.

Fourth, God inserts important notes not found other places in the text. Here are a couple of examples. One of these you may be familiar; the other, probably not. Several years ago the little book *The Prayer of Jabez: Breaking Through to the Blessed Life* [10] by Bruce Wilkerson was published and became the rave. Many Christians began praying the three millennium old prayer Jabez lifted to God. [11] Through Jabez, God taught what it meant when He blessed, i.e., increase, expansion without duress. He taught us it was reserved for only honorable people. Another break in the record occurs, connected with the account of Abraham's beginnings in Ur. It is in the Tenth Chapter when it mentions Peleg. In the account is this curious statement: in the lifetime of Peleg the earth was divided. [12] Peleg's name means *division*. Does it mean divisions of places for Noah's sons to settle? Or, does it mean the original land of Eden, inferring that until Peleg's time there was only one known continent and it divided? I will leave those two with you.

But we need to get back to Ur or I run the risk you won't remember that this chapter concerns the sea change of events beginning with President Obama and the corresponding disasters. We resume with the timeline. In doing so, I hope you were enlightened by what you have read since we left a summary of the events catalogued in *Eye To Eye: Facing the Consequences of Dividing Israel*. [7]

January 20, 2009

On January 20, 2009, Barak Hussein Obama takes the Oath of Office and becomes the 44th President of the United States. Prior to his election, there was apprehension among some American supporters of Israel because of Candidate Obama's association with PLO ideologue Rashid Khalidi and the anti-Semitic Rev. Jeremiah Wright. Once into the campaign, his speeches reflected strong support for Israel.

April 19, 2009

Within three months, almost to the day he was sworn into office, on April 19, 2009, President Obama states during a news conference at the Hilton Hotel, Port of Spain, Trinidad and Tobago [13] that the United States intends to join the United Nations' Human Rights Council (HRC). The Huffington Post reports the HRC is "… a body widely criticized for failing to confront abuses around the world and for acting primarily to condemn Israel." [14] This move will come to prove disastrous for America, as we shall see later.

April 19, 2010

Exactly one year later, April 19, 2010, Fox News reports a shift in US policy toward Israel in the United Nations Security Council. The report explains the United States no longer intends to use its veto power when certain (unspecified) anti-Israeli issues come to a vote. Historically, the United States has been the defender of Israel on scurrilous anti-Israeli issues. [15]

April 20, 2010

One day later, on Monday, April 20, 2010, an oil rig operated by British Petroleum blows out in the Gulf of Mexico. Days pass before the well can be capped. Millions of gallons of oil contaminate the waters wrecking property damage and financial havoc to the Gulf Coast's people and sea life. Over one hundred fifty lawsuits were filed.

The Deep Water Horizon, the name of the rig, took eighty—seven days to cap. During that time, 4.9 million barrels or 210 million US gallons erupted into the water. Numbers this large are very difficult, if not impossible, for the human mind to comprehend. It would fill about 14 million gas tanks of the average American car. It is still too big. It would fill four and a half oil refinery storage tanks. There, that is a comprehendible number. Deep Water Horizon's infamy is it is the largest oil spill in the petroleum industry's history. After burning, the rig sunk. [16]

May 19, 2011

Another year passes. It is May 19, 2011. The president publically states Israel must return to pre-1967 borders. [17] United States national policy toward Israel shifts negatively once again with another hard turn. This declaration, if implemented, essentially strips Israel of any warning of a military attack by her Arab Islamist enemies. Remember how small a footprint of land Israel now has; about the size of the State of New Jersey. In today's modern warfare, a warning of attack on that small a country is reduced to bare minutes. Push Israel back to the pre-1967 borders and it becomes seconds. Most certainly, it proves her inability to defend herself. Permitting land to be taken away from her is not acceptable under the promises of the covenant.

May 22, 2011

May 22, 2011 is a day of tornados tearing east across the heartland of America. An F5 tornado drops out of the sky just west of Joplin, Missouri. Directly in its mile wide path is the city itself. Joplin is ravaged. By the time of the Joplin tornado, watchers of television news were at risk of being numbed to the sights of disasters shown in video footage. The scenes and reports from Joplin were somehow different; somehow closer to home for most of us, though most had never been there. There may have been a good reason for that. And, it was on a spiritual level.

There are astounding correlations to the Joplin tornado and Israel. The correlations:

- Center of the Western World's focus is on Israel, particularly Jerusalem. Israel is the apple (focus) of God's attention. The

- geographical center of America is Missouri. It is also the broadest representation of America's culture according to Wikipedia. It is quintessential America.
- Joplin comes from a word meaning Job according to Ancestry.com. President Obama's demand struck at Israel's existence with his demand for pre—1967 borders. Job's existence was also threatened and he suffered devastating loss. Joplin suffered devastation and deaths that could easily spelled her death as a city. Had it not been for the flood of help and assistance from those who were distant from Joplin, she may have been much less of a city. Compassion of the American people was the victor of devastation. Compassion from God saved Job.
- The president's demand also struck at the Jerusalem of biblical times, called the Old City, which was captured by the Jews in the 1967 War. Its population is about 50,000. Joplin's population is about 50,000.

Our national policy of turning from Israel has heightened the severity of disasters.

September 11, 2011

The tenth anniversary of the infamous day in 2001 arrives on the calendar; 9/11. Though there is some anxiety on the part of some,

Chapter Two: Disasters

Americans approach the day with little fear. Then, the news bulletins begin about an attack in Libya on one of our consulates. Later in the day, we all learn our ambassador and three other Americans are killed. Sovereign American territory is under attack again. Now, it is the US Consulate in Benghazi, Libya. The attack is allegedly by Islamic terrorists affiliated with the same group of the attack in September 11, 2001. Ambassador J. Christopher Stevens and three other American citizens lose their lives. Eleven years to the day, fire again destroys American property and takes American lives. God's warning is almost a shout it is so clear: America, without repentance from your policy toward Israel, a fiery curse is yet to come on you. The ultimate response will not be a consulate burning down, rather the seat of your government being destroyed and with it, the way of life you have known.

September 27, 2012

Israeli Prime Minister Benjamin Netanyahu calls for the United States to draw a line — a Red Line he calls it — concerning the point at which military action will be taken against Iran should her nuclear weapons program continue. Netanyahu spoke during a news conference in Jerusalem and later at the United Nations General Assembly. There was no response from the Obama administration then or later. To minds of the Middle East, this type of public call and the return of silence is a message of approval to continue. The unstated silence to Middle Easterners: Israel you are on your own and will suffer the consequences of your actions on your own. Israel is a Middle Eastern country. They heard the same, unspoken message.

October 25, 2012

Another year passes. On October 25, 2012, the Washington Free Beacon publishes an article revealing the HRC is releasing a report calling for an international campaign of legal attacks and economic warfare on a group of American and European companies that do business in Israel. The Drudge Report, the online news agency equal in readership to the New York Times picks the story up and provides a link. The report warns American employees of the targeted companies that they face personal, legal risks of human rights violations. [18] Effectively, through the United Nations the United States government plans to wage legal war on American companies who do business in Israel through citizens whom the companies employ. Effects of this action, if implemented, will leave Israel isolated politically, damaged financially and weakened militarily. In such a condition, she cannot survive, 1967 borders notwithstanding. She, in time, will become too weak to defend herself.

We have been traveling the timeline of history. Now, we come to the most sobering and ominous warning of all. It is precipitated by this deceptive change in our policy. The pattern now changes from the model Bill Koenig has been following. No longer is the warning of God directed at the United States for our co-conspiracy with Israel's enemies to that part of her land in a naive, myopic quest for peace. Now it is about our membership in the United Nations' Human Rights Council. The warning is precipitated through a report concerning the Human Rights Council's intention to bypass land for peace and go for a knockout, guised in political correctness; the annihilation of Israel as a nation. The spirit of antichrist is finally revealed. His work since 1991 comes into focus. If he can destroy the covenant, he destroys God's legitimacy and authority. What follows is what I warned about proving to be disastrous earlier in the section under March, 2009.

October 3, 2012

Super Storm Sandy comes ashore in New Jersey. It is October 30, 2012. It is the eleventh anniversary of the Perfect Storm. Descriptions of her destruction are described as being of biblical proportions. One might stop and wonder if Super Storm Sandy were targeted at the United Nations headquarters in New York City. Sure, it matters the United Nations is located in New York City and the storm did great damage to the city; however, twenty—one states suffered great damage. The United States was the target. And once again, the east coast from Washington, D.C. to New York City.

The message of Wall Street should not be overlooked. Historically, Wall Street was named because of a wall built to protect lower Manhattan Island from flood waters from an overflowing canal (now Canal Street). Flood waters did come into the New York Stock Exchange during Super Storm Sandy. Could this be a sign America's financial strength is about to be drowned?

Until we joined the UN Human Rights Council they had no leverage. Now, they have the United States of America as a full-fledged co–conspirator against Israel. Desire without means is of little practical value. Means and desire become a force with which to be reckoned. The United States has effectively weaponized Islamist nations politically through the United Nations against Israel. And, it was all done under the umbrella of political correctness. Yet, the United States still claims to be Israel's staunchest ally. Israel is fast running out of friends.

Please do not pass this important fact. It is of no coincidence the two storms, The Perfect Storm and Super Storm Sandy occur on the same day. Nor is it no coincidence the first did some damage and the second storm that of biblical proportions. The circle closed. The warnings will continue for an allotted time to allow for repentance to seek mercy and then the curse of judgment will fall.

The Wrap

We have covered a lot of dates and a lot of corresponding events, with Rabbit Trails in between. Events up until 9/11 were disasters, but all were of a more local nature. All were connected with land for peace. Things changed with 9/11. It is though God is saying you've taken the wrong path. It will lead to your sure judgment and consequences that will not compare with this. Steadily, our distance away from support for Israel became greater; more threatening to her land and her security. Whereas before, there was the support as a friend to Israel on one hand; on the other, our self-desire for economic security, based on free flowing oil at market prices, caused us to act in a way as to add air to the fire of Middle East antagonism toward her.

All the while, our society continues moral decay. It became obvious to me during the Vietnam War. I am sure there are scholars who pinpoint the date with accuracy. As I began to reflect on the times, I was reminded of Shuttle Diplomacy, first under President Nixon during the 1970's. Each trip by Henry Kissinger to the Middle East made the national news. And it made him a household name. And the efforts continued under Presidents Ford, Carter and

Reagan. Under President George H. W. Bush our informal policy turned formal.

So, as we sent emissaries to the Middle East to try and bring peace that would assure stabilized oil prices, we unwittingly acted like a god in the region. In doing so, our society began to pull away from the true God. God pulled away from us just as the other side of the written Rule would imply: draw near to God and He will draw near to you.[19] The obvious unwritten point is that He won't force the drawing together. We pulled away from God, He pulled away from us. I do not believe, as some, that this moral decay is the cause of our coming judgment. Robert Bork's *Slouching toward Gomorra: Modern Liberalism and the American Decline* [20] eloquently and accurately, in my opinion, warned America that our country's path was not leading us toward Bethlehem; rather, Gomorra. Judge Bork was correct, but God doesn't judge nations on their collective morality. He judges the individuals of those nations. Individuals will stand judgment for their rebellion against God's instructions as how people are to live their lives. He judges nations as to how they treat Israel. This is about Israel, the blessing and the curse. It is about His covenant obligation.

I cannot emphasis to strongly how serious our policy and our actions toward Israel are to God. As a people, we generally see

Chapter Two: Disasters

ourselves as Israel's friend. I am tempted to go into a foreign policy discussion, but it is too late for that and that is not what this book is about. It is about why God's judgment is about to fall on us. In that regard, the table on the following table sums up our actions.

MESSAGES OR COINCIDENCES?
1991 TO 2012

DATE	POLITICAL EVENT	WARNING
October 30, 1991	Madrid Conference	The Perfect Storm
September 11, 2001	President George W Bush promise public announcement of support for Palestinian state	Islamic terrorist attack America
1991–'2004	Events outlined in *Eye to Eye: Facing the Consequences of Dividing Israel*	
April 19, 2010	USA will no longer automatically veto UN Security Council Resolutions unfriendly to Israel	
April 20, 2010		*Deep Water Horizon* blows in Gulf of Mexico
May 19, 2011	President Obama states Israel must return to 1967 borders	
May 22, 2011		F5 tornado strikes Joplin, MO
September 11, 2011		US Consulate attacked in Benghazi, Libya. Ambassador and two other Americans killed

September 12, 2011	Israeli Prime Minister publically pressures President Obama to "draw a Red Line" over Iranian nuclear production	
October 25, 2012	UN Human Rights Council announces plan to punish employees of American and British companies doing business in Israel	
October 30, 2012		Super Storm Sandy ravishes NE coastline of US

If it has escaped your notice, God is a God of circles, or cycles. It is reflected throughout creation. Nature is our laboratory to test the hypothesis. Galleries revolve in the universe. Our sun revolves around the center of our Milky Way in approximately 225 million years. You know about the calculation of years and days. Atoms have nucleuses and revolving electrons. Life itself is a cycle. It goes on and on. Repeating cycles are a pattern of the Bible. Players change, the story changes and yet, the teaching points remain consistent: mankind has failed to honor God, thus, mankind's future is one of doom, only God can save mankind, He does so without violating man's free will, those not accepting God's salvation will be eternally separated from God following God's judgment. In telling and retelling, all returns to its beginning point and then a new cycle begins. A cycle completes, a new cycle begins. And so it is here.

Chapter Two: Disasters

Warnings began with a storm on October 30, 1991. They ended with a storm on October 30, 2012. The cycle for warning is finished. It was not heeded, now comes the cycle to beg for mercy in the face of the sure, coming judgment. That will be the subject opened in our next chapter.

Sometime around 2004, God revealed to me seven verses of prophetic scripture. They speak to the United States of America. These seven verses partially answer the questions of why, what and when concerning our coming judgment; yet, as through the darkened glass. So, come and find America in the Bible.

CHAPTER THREE: THE UNNAMED NATION

The cause of our judgment summarized in six words

Bible students have asked since the World Wars if the United States — the most powerful nation on earth — is in the Bible. The reasoning is that our world is entering or has entered what is known as the last days. It is only logical the USA would be a player in the so—called end time's scenario. Some have speculated that we are one of the young lions (or villages) of the merchants of Tarshish referred to in Ezekiel 38:13 or the eagle of Revelation 12:13-17. Or perhaps, we are Babylon the Great. America is not mentioned by name, so if these are the last days or the end times, how can America, the most powerful nation on earth, not be involved in the most astounding days of mankind? The Lord has shown me why and it is my job to share it with you.

Proverbs, like every other book in the Bible is filled with wonderful truths. For me, Proverbs is a most special book. The number

Chapter Three: The Unnamed Nation

of chapters of Proverbs equals the number of days of the month and thus, suggests it is intended as a monthly reading plan. Proverbs is full of obvious and hidden practical applications for how to live a life pleasing to God. It is also filled with wonderful mysteries. A most memorable experience of this revelation, or teaching by the Holy Spirit, is found in one of Proverbs' verses. It is Proverbs 25:2 and it reads, "It is the glory of God to conceal a matter, but the glory of kings is to search out a matter." [21] Does that sound too mysterious? Well, here is the magic.

- The word *glory* in Hebrew means the manifestation of God's presence in our physical realm. To the Jew, that also has the connotation of blessing; positive increase, a benefit.
- The word translated *to conceal* means to hide, but with the idea that someone will come to find what is hidden.
- *Kings* is a group of sovereign rulers over their separate kingdoms. The implication here is a king's rule benefits from or is enhanced by this search the writer is talking about.
- *Search* in the Hebrew doesn't mean just to look for something. It means when you think you have found it, to dig it up. In their day, there were no banks. Money was in the form of coins. For safe keeping then, they would bury their money on property they owned.

- And finally, the word *matter*. It can mean a thing, but its first meaning is word(s).

With these meanings in mind, let me re-render the verse. *It is a benefit from God to hide His word so that it can be found, and it is the benefit to those who are royal rulers to dig up this word.* Do you see the marvel of it? God's word, our Bible, is like a field. In it is hidden a greater wealth about Him and His ways than that which we receive from just a surface reading. Isn't that neat? Oh yes, a certain Rabbi from Nazareth had a teaching which further revealed this truth. He said, "The kingdom of heaven is like a treasure hidden in the field, which a man found and hid *again;* and from joy over it he goes and sells all that he has and buys that field." [22]

So, it was that secret hidden in Proverbs that let me see what the Holy Spirit had to teach me about this particular prophecy. It has been said that prophecy is the news of the future. What an arresting statement. No doubt news and prophecy both capture the interest and attention of most of us. Early in my Christian walk I read Hal Lindsey's book, *The Late Great Planet Earth,* as I shared in the Introduction. As I now remember, I watched with eagerness for the events to unfold. They did not, at least the way I understood they would. To say Mr. Lindsey was wrong is to be disingenuous. Because of his book there are numbers, known only to God, of human hearts

Chapter Three: The Unnamed Nation

softened and made ready to receive the words of faith for believing the reward of salvation.

Whether this message will so touch another is not for me to know. Nor do I claim any gift in what follows. I have no credentials which give the weight of authority. I believe when it comes to the subject of biblical prophecy, one has only the revelation of understanding given from God. There are no scholarly degrees; ordinations of man or the following of devotees who confer the touch of God. Several years ago God gave me a glimpse into what Isaiah was prophesying. I don't make the claim that I have the definitive account of this yet future story. I admit what follows may well sound to you like that of a voice in the wilderness; I am alone in what I am about to say. Few scholars would agree with my premise that Isaiah 18 is spoken to the United States of America and this generation.

Biblical prophecy is a fascinating magnet while at the same time confusing. It is my invitation we sit together as students with open minds, inviting and allowing God's Spirit of Truth to be our teacher. Should He show you something He has not shown me, please share it. If you are willing, then let's begin.

For the convenience of reference, Appendix A has the verses of Isaiah 18 from several translations. Most verses in the text are from

New American Standard Version (1995). If not your preference, I hope your favorite translation is in the Appendix.

Isaiah — God's Unique Oracle

The Man

He, like most men of his time, stood about five feet tall. Every male he knew had facial hair. Isaiah's position in the Jewish society was not the norm. Scholarly understanding is that Isaiah was a member of the royal court. This meant he had a most exalted position in society. It is my belief God set him in this position because of the extensive, important prophetic message for which he was commissioned concerning the Messiah. As John the Baptist was of the House of Aaron, thus qualified from the priestly line to anoint Jesus; Isaiah, as a member of the court is granted proclamation as to the nature of the coming Messiah first as servant and then king.

Isaiah had a 64 year ministry from the 7th into the 8th Century B.C. In his end, things did not turn out well for Isaiah. Faithful to God in the performance of his office, he was found to be an enemy of the court. Tradition holds, from two sources outside the Bible (*Martyrdom of Isaiah*[23] and the *Lives of the Prophets*[24]), his violent end came on the Mount of Olives where he was martyred by King Manasseh over his opposition to pagan worship.

Chapter Three: The Unnamed Nation

His Time

Isaiah lived following King Solomon's reign during the period of the divided kingdom. It was the time of prophets; many more of them than we are familiar with from the biblical account. The others spoke to the immediate future of their times as do ours of today. Those names which we know had the common thread of speaking also of the Messiah's future advents and reign. Of them all, Isaiah was preeminent. Through him, God was not only warning about a sure coming judgment were there no repentance while at the same time giving evidence of His coming mission as a suffering servant and then, as King of the whole world.

His Message to the Nations

Isaiah 18 falls into a section of his work known as the Woe Chapters. The word *woe* in Hebrew is the word *hoy*. *Hoy* is translated as *ah*, *alas* and *dead*. This distinctive form of prophetic speech is often found accompanying an accusation or threat which immediately preceded an announcement of judgment. [25] The word implies coming doom; it can also be seen as a warning to repent. The message is to the nations who surround Israel today, all of whom want her to cease to exist. Their plan to accomplish this is to first weaken her people through terrorism, burdening them with constant fear and to reduce the amount of land she has for her defense. This is guised in the oft hear phrase land for peace. They were enemies of Israel in Isaiah's day, as well. Isaiah names them as he knew them. (Many Bibles have maps of the periods in the Old Testament which, along with the woe chapters, one can identify the countries to whom Isaiah speaks.) Each chapter names the country singled out, all are named but one. Isaiah did not know this nation, so he described it from what God showed him.

The WOW in the Beginning of the Woe Chapters

Chapter 14

The beginning of woes is when Israel enters her rest. *Rest* in Hebrew here means to rest, settle down, and remain. In the vernacular: you have arrived at the place of your home, so settle here. I believe Isaiah is speaking of the time beginning on May 14, 1948 when, in one day (as scripture stated [26]), Israel was declared a nation. One's natural response to this assertion is, why would it be this date from all other dates? Why couldn't it just as easily be the previous year when the UN voted to approve statehood for Israelis and the Palestinians? Here is why and here begins the WOW.

Ezekiel 4:4, 5

I am indebted to the Alpha News Daily web site for what follows. [27] They may be found at http://www.alphanewsdaily.com.

This bewildering command is given to Ezekiel: As for you, lie down on your left side and lay the iniquity of the house of Israel on

Chapter Three: The Unnamed Nation

it; you shall bear their iniquity for the number of days that you lie on it. For I have assigned you a number of days corresponding to the years of their iniquity, three hundred and ninety days; thus you shall bear the iniquity of the house of Israel. When you have completed these, you shall lie down a second time, *but* on your right side and bear the iniquity of the house of Judah; I have assigned it to you for forty days, a day for each year." [28]

Here is a quick background update. Contrary to what many believe, Solomon did not serve God; rather, himself. After his death the kingdom was divided. Israel became the northern kingdom; Judah the southern. Two kingdoms made up the one nation. All the kings of Israel behaved badly, as did half the kings of Judah. The iniquity Ezekiel is bearing in the above scripture refers to their sin as kings by failing to observe the Sabbatical Year. All under God's Instruction (Law) were to rest one day out of seven and one year out of seven, as well. Israel had not observed a Sabbath Year for 390 years; Judah 40 years. This year was known as the Shmitah year. As a nation they were guilty of 430 years. It is the years of guilt of the nation that is important. Because the kings (leaders) were guilty, their subjects were as well. This rule has not changed.

The Northern Kingdom was taken into captivity and dispersed among the nations. These are known as the 10 lost tribes of Israel — a gross misnomer. They were never lost to God. The Southern Kingdom, on the other hand, was taken into captivity by the Babylonians in 606 B.C. for 70 years. That leaves 360 years unaccounted. Now, watch this!

Bible scholars could not find any specific captivity or dispersion that fulfilled these 360 years left in the judgment *until* a close look in the book of Leviticus revealed a *startling* prophetic warning:

"And after all this, if you do not obey Me, then I (God) will punish you *seven times more* for your sins."

(Leviticus 26:18)

"Then, if you walk contrary to Me, and are not willing to obey Me, I (God) will bring on you seven times more plagues, according to your sins."

(Leviticus 26:21)

"And after all this, if you do not obey Me, but walk contrary to Me, then I (God) also will walk contrary to you in fury; and I, even I will chastise you seven times for your sins."

(Leviticus 26:27-28)

"I (God) will scatter you among the nations and draw a sword after you; your Land shall be desolate and your cities waste."

(Leviticus 26:33)

Chapter Three: The Unnamed Nation

God warned Israel in four separate scriptures that if they continued in their disobedience to His instructions to them, He would multiply the length of their disobedience by seven times in their judgment!

So, let's see how this factor of seven works out.

360 Remaining years of judgment

x 7 The prophetic 7 factor

= 2,520 Years of judgment remained against Israel

God gave the Jews the most sophisticated calendar on Earth. It is both a lunar *and* a solar calendar. We call it the Jewish calendar. What a deceitful trick by Satan. It is God's calendar. It uses a 360 day lunar year and then adds a 'Leap Month' on specific years to accurately coincide with the solar cycle which is used by our Gregorian calendar. The 360 days are God's reckoning for a year, so in prophecy using 365 days won't work out.

The Bible uses 360 day years for prophecies and expects us to add the appropriate leap months on schedule. So, the easiest way to unravel this prophecy is to first convert this prophecy into days.

2,520 years

x 360 days

= 907,200 days of judgment remain against nation Israel after the Babylonian captivity

Now, to convert the 907,200 days found in the prophecy into our 365.25 day years, including leap years.

907,200 days

÷ **365.25** days

= 2,483.78 years remain

Now, let's look at the prophecy again.

-606 B.C. Israel taken into Babylonian captivity

- 70 Years for the 70 years of captivity

-536 B.C. End of first 70 years of judgment (because they are B.C. years, a minus sign is in the equation)

+2484 Years (we rounded off the years of remaining judgment. By adding it to the minus B.C. years we move forward on the timeline to...)

= 1948 A.D.!

This ends of the judgment against the nation Israel. She begins her rest as she begins her statehood. Remember, rest means the place one is supposed to be; the place to settle. It does not mean peace.

What makes this mathematical Bible prophecy even more remarkable is this. Take this same prophetic timeline (which starts in the year of Babylon's conquest of the nation Israel and ends with Israel once again raised as a nation in 1948) and shift it to begin instead with the year Babylon returned and destroyed Jerusalem.

This happened 19 years after the conquest. Remarkably, this prophetic timeline's end—point now falls on the exact year Israel once again took sovereign control over Jerusalem in 1967 during the Six Day War.

Many Jewish Rabbis believe this is the beginning of Jacob's Trouble (for Christians: the End Times). It is not the beginning of the tribulation taught in the Book of Revelation.

Woe Chapters, Ezekiel and Isaiah 18

The Woe Chapters tell of Israel's enemies and their judgment at the hand of God.

Somewhere along the timeline, following the Six Day War, are the prophecies in these chapters fulfilled. All of these nations desire to take Israel's land. They do not want part of her land for a Palestinian state. They could have had a state several different times over the years, beginning with the United Nations declaration in 1947 awarding Israel statehood. That was not and has never been their purpose, only a ploy.

The nation in Isaiah 18, as we shall see, is a co-conspirator with the other nations. This nation is not an enemy in the sense of aggression, rather as an enabler or co—conspirator, as it were, to help the aggressors achieve their aim of taking Israel's land and thus, voiding God's covenant. His covenant voided would be His word voided and then He would not be God over this realm; Satan would. God cannot let this stand. So, who is this co—conspirator nation? Let's look with Isaiah and see what he saw.

Isaiah 18 -- Clues to the Un-named Nation

Verse 1

Alas, oh land of whirring wings which lies beyond the rivers of Cush, [29]

The first word is a distinctive form of prophetic speech often found accompanying an accusation or threat which immediately precedes an announcement of judgment. Often it is used in funeral dirges. The NET Bible translates it *as good as dead*.

Imagine living in 500 B.C. E. and in a vision seeing a major airport, like Dulles International. Planes are taking off, landing, taxing. Engines on the wings are obviously the source of the whine your ears hear. How would you describe it? Translations differ, but all convey the connection of sound and wings.

Next comes the most important identifier; it is the key to this chapter. It is the word *beyond*. It is the Hebrew word *min*. This word can be translated among, but the strong sense of its meaning is beyond — on the other side. The Chronicle Project [30] renders *min* "that to pass across". In this case pass across the rivers of Cush to the destination. Cush in biblical times was present day Ethiopia and

Chapter Three: The Unnamed Nation

Southern Sudan. The following map shows approximately the area of ancient Cush.

THE RIVERS OF CUSH

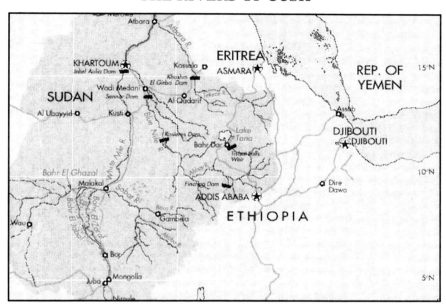

The rivers to which Isaiah refers are the head waters of the Blue Nile. Find the word *Sudan* on the map, to the right is *Wadi Medani* and just to the right of that is the confluence of two rivers into the Blue Nile. The map does not show the topography, but this whole area is just west of a mountainous divide and a part of the western slope. These head waters into the Blue Nile join with the White Nile, as you can see, to the northwest to form the Nile. These headwaters are the rivers of Cush. The revelation here is the direction these rivers point. If Isaiah only meant the direction was just on the other side of the rivers, without regard for a specific azimuth, he most likely would have referred to the Nile, itself; a much more recognizable landmark. Since he refers to the rivers of Cush, there must be a reason and I believe it is the direction in which they point. The idea then, to find the unnamed nation, one must follow the direction the rivers point before they begin to merge and turn North. That is exactly what the map below shows.

THE RIVERS OF CUSH POINT TO THE UNNAMED NATION

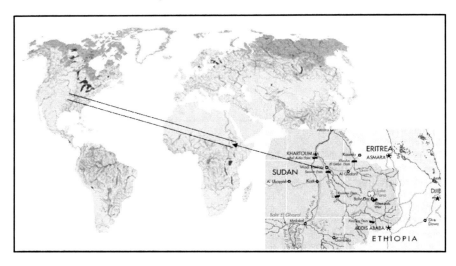

This map is not meant to be exact. It cannot be done on this scale, at least by me. When the Holy Spirit showed me this, I was in a church that I didn't go to and was there only twice for a Bible study. In the hallway between the classroom and the rest room, there was a very large map of the world on the wall. The Holy Spirit

Chapter Three: The Unnamed Nation

had just recently educated me that the rivers were very important to Isaiah's prophecy. The first time I was there I checked Ethiopia and found these rivers. All the other rivers I could find in Ethiopia were singular. It looked to me that they did point to America, but it was a large map. When I returned the next week, I had a cloth tape measure with me; I laid it over the rivers, held it firmly in place and unrolled it. It unrolled directly across the middle of the continental United States. I don't have the vocabulary to accurately describe what I felt.

You will see that I have added a Rabbit Trail just below the next paragraph. It is not the normal Rabbit Trail. This one is to expound on Cush. For many, the above explanation is sufficient and you are ready to move to Verse Two, below. You may do that at any time you feel comfortable that the Cush to which Isaiah refers is today's Southern Sudan and Ethiopia. In the Rabbit Trail, I am going to be dealing with the minutiae surrounding the identity of Cush's location and the people known as Cushites among scholars.

I am doing this because there will be detractors of this book. Every Christian book in which a controversial subject is raised will, in turn, raise detractors. Since the phrase *beyond the rivers of Cush* is the lynchpin identifying the unnamed nation, this will be among the first points to be assaulted. I want to offer a pre-emptive rebuttal.

To be clear, I am not referring to a well-reasoned critique. Those are certainly proper. The difference is the tone and substance of what is written: mean spirited and limited as to the facts. These kinds of criticisms are invariably clothed in the guise of defending God's word. In reality, they are usually no more than the defense of the writer's own position. The defense of the faith is defending the truth of the life, death and resurrection of Jesus; what He taught, what He said, what He did. I do not believe these writers are bad people. I believe they are spiritually immature and don't know it. Later in the book, I will deal with how to tell where one is in the Christian walk, or where in the development of spiritual maturity. The kind of spiritual immaturity I speak is not unlike the predictable out lash when a Christian leader's sin is made public. How quickly, seemingly pious people within the Church, devour him; as a pack of wild animals would a fallen prey. Of course, I am not condoning Sin, but I am not condoning this kind of response to it, either. Enough! Here is the Rabbit Trail on Cush.

Rabbit Trail #1

Back into the mists of time, the second of Noah's three sons was named Ham. He had four sons. They were Cush, Misraim, Put and Canaan. Since the three younger brothers are also the names of places, I am assuming Cush is as well. I am also agreeing with those

Chapter Three: The Unnamed Nation

who think Ham's name is entomologically related to the words for *warm* and *hot*. This supposition leads to the assumption that Ham settled in the hotter lands of the ancient world. The Anchor Yale Bible Dictionary suggests that Misraim is Egypt, Put is either Libya or the Horn of Africa (I vote Libya because of prophecy), Canaan from Lebanon to the Nile and Cush, father of the Cushites. (Oh my, that is not a place.) Cush also had sons, the most infamous being Nimrod which gives him a Mesopotamian (Iraq) connection. So, after all of that, where is Cush where Cushites live?

Genesis 25: 1—6 tells us Abraham took a wife named Keturah and had sons. Before he died, he bequeathed them gifts sending them out of Canaan to the east, away from Isaac. One of these sons was named Midian. His supposed descendants, the Midianites, we find in the Joseph accounts. They are traders with Egypt from Gilead, an area in what is now Jordan. Fast forward to Moses where we find he fled after killing the Egyptian and comes to Midian, living with Jethro and marrying his daughter, Zipporah. But, in Numbers 12:1, we find out Moses' wife was a Cushite. I am assuming this is Zipporah, because the Bible is very focused on entomologies. No other wife is ever mentioned for Moses, the greatest Jew next to Jesus. If he had more than one wife, I am confident we would know of her. Ezekiel the Tragedian, in a non—biblical work, has Zipporah, describing herself to Moses, as being a stranger in Midian. She says that she is from Libya, a land inhabited by various peoples, including Ethiopians — dark men. Later, the Prophet Jeremiah asks in 13:23, "Can the Ethiopian change his skin or the leopard his stripes?" My last reference is from Josephus in his *Antiquities of the Jews*. In 6:1, he makes this statement:

For of the four sons of Ham, time has not at all hurt the name of Cush; for the Ethiopians, over whom he reigned, are even at this day, both by themselves and by all men in Asia, called Cushites? It would not appear Cush is in Asia, rather the ancient land of Ethiopia.

There is not enough historical record to prove Cush, the land to which Isaiah was referring, is where I have set it, on the other hand there is far less of a record to prove otherwise. This would be the land now known as South Sudan, Ethiopia, Eretria, and Djibouti. (Part of Ethiopia has also been known as Abyssinia.)

If this were the only clue Isaiah left us to identify the unnamed nation, a very weak argument could be made that the rivers of Cush point to another geographical location. Fortunately, it is not the only clue. True to the biblical pattern, everything is confirmed by two or three witnesses, or testimonies of truth.

Verse 2

>...*which sends envoys by the sea, even in papyrus vessels on the surface of the waters. Go, swift*

Chapter Three: The Unnamed Nation

messengers, to a nation tall and smooth, to a people feared far and wide, a powerful and oppressive nation whose land the rivers divide. [31]

Identifying the unnamed nation is not unlike following a trail of crumbs. Isaiah has told us the direction in which to look for the nation, he now describes the most telltale thing about the conduct of the nation as it relates to Israel. To Isaiah, this is the most important thing he has to say so it comes first. In Hebrew, what comes first is preeminent. In six words, the reason God must judge America is summarized. Envoys, emissaries if you will, are sent by way of the sea.

> *...which sends envoys by the sea, even in papyrus vessels on the surface of the waters. Go, swift messengers, to a nation tall and smooth, to a people feared far and wide, a powerful and oppressive nation whose land the rivers divide.*
> Isaiah 18: 2

If one knows the envoys' mission, one can understand the prophecy.

Isaiah thinks it important to point out two facts about this sea journey. To Isaiah, they must have seemed beyond strange. First, the envoys were in papyrus vessels. Along the Nile, of which Isaiah would be familiar, the plentiful papyrus plant would be pounded into sheets and applied over the hulls of boats. The hull therefore gave the appearance of panels. If Isaiah were looking at a jet in flight, the riveted panels may have well reminded him of the Nile boats. Well and good, but why would he point out they were on the surface of the waters? Where else would a sea going vessel be in 500 B.C.? But, if it were a jet airplane it would be over the surface. This thing he sees is not a bird. He heard the whirring wings at the airport. It is a craft in which people ride. Yet how can it fly like a bird and not flap its wings? How does Isaiah comprehend all of this and then describe it? He describes what he sees closest to what he knows.

Another perplexity arises. Who are the swift messengers and who tells them to go? Throughout scripture messengers (sent ones) refer to angels. Isaiah heard the command given to angels. They have a message to deliver to our unnamed nation. In so doing, he returns to more descriptions to identify the angels' addressee.

The people are described physically, how peoples of other nations view them, how other governments view them and finally, a physical identifier.

1. A people tall and smooth, the Hebrew is actually translated *drawn out*, may well mean people noticeably taller than Isaiah's frame of five feet. Isaiah most likely did not know a man who was clean shaven. To describe them he said drawn out and smooth.

2. These people are feared by all. Why? Perhaps the clue is next.

Chapter Three: The Unnamed Nation

3. The nation is powerful. It has the military and economic power to enforce its will. And, if challenged, it does not hesitate to do so.
4. Finally, it is a nation divided by rivers. America is essentially divided by the Ohio and Missouri merging to form the Mississippi. America is a nation divided by rivers.
5. Isaiah does not say anything about their color. Ethiopians were noted in the Bible as having dark skin, as we have seen. This being the most distinguishing description about Ethiopians is almost always noted in other writings, its absence would strongly indicate Isaiah is not referring to Ethiopians. This substantially weakens any conclusion this prophecy is for the nation of Ethiopia.

Isaiah's pointers and descriptions are complete. All of the puzzle pieces are known. Assembled, the picture becomes clear and understandable.

The Name of Isaiah's Unnamed Nation

The nation would not have a name for 2,300 years. Isaiah observed a moment in time of this nation's future when it exerts its will against Israel and becomes a co—conspirator with Israel's enemies. Let's go through the exercise and find the nation once again, based on what Isaiah has told us. Imagine with me a globe of the world. Now, take a ribbon just wide enough to cover the rivers of Ethiopia. Now, holding the ribbon in place, stretch it around the globe. If the direction of Ethiopia's rivers is followed around the globe, they lead to the middle of the United States of America! For the most part, the men who conduct the nation's business are clean shaven and tall, compared to men of 500 B.C. Our nation is blessed with navigable rivers. The largest ones act as dividers of the land.

Though we think of ourselves as peace loving it doesn't mean others do, particularly those nations of the Middle East during the timeframe when Isaiah's message applies. When is this moment in time that Isaiah is witness? Isaiah told us. It is the time when we send emissaries to the Middle East. Our interest in the region began in earnest under the Nixon administration with "shuttle diplomacy." Make no mistake about the fact this involvement has always been about our oil imports. A peaceful Middle East means stable oil prices and continuity of delivery. It was not until the Madrid Peace Conference in 1991 did our policy of Israel's land in exchange for a stable peace take the form of official national policy. We are acting in what we believe is our and the worlds' best interest: stable oil prices. The path we have taken to accomplish this aim has caused us to collude with Israel's enemies to take land. For us, we assume it will secure peace; for them, a weakened Israel. In both cases, God's covenant is challenged and that puts the United States on the wrong side of God.

The Messenger's Message

The message the Messengers (angels) are sent to deliver is to stop our policy of trying to forge a Middle East peace by coercing Israel to relinquish their covenant land. The previous chapters gave a complete accounting of how this message was delivered and how it was received. Every time we squeezed Israel diplomatically, we experienced a corresponding storm, usually natural, but sometimes economic or political. It was from the Messengers.

None of Isaiah's prophecy could have possibly been understood until well after 1991. Bible commentaries will not identify the US as the unnamed nation because until only very recently has America fulfilled all of the Isaiah's qualifications. This is why I said earlier that what scholars wrote in the past would not be in agreement with my premise. It is just too recent to fit their paradigm.

CHAPTER FOUR: THE BAD NEWS

It was spoken, it was written, it will come to pass

Isaiah 18 — Prophecy and Judgment

Verse 3

All you inhabitants of the world and dwellers on earth, as soon as a standard is raised on the mountains, you will see it, and as soon as the trumpet is blown, you will hear it. [32]

This verse is packed with suggested meaning. At first glance, it is obviously an announcement to the world the coming event will be news, really big news. It is comparable to 9/11 in the kind of coverage it will initially receive. It is the announcement of an event which will cause a sea change in the world's power alignment. In Isaiah's time, armies would mass for battle and look to higher ground for the signal from their commander to attack. A banner, standard or flag, would be raised for all the army to see and with it a trumpet blast. The attack would begin. Thus, it is very clear this is not strategic, as was 9/11 and Pearl Harbor. This is an all-out assault on the country. People will understand what they are witnessing is devastation beyond man's capability.

Two sets of descriptions in the verse capture one's attention. They go beyond what they seem at first glance. They are:

1. *inhabitants* of the *world*
2. *dwellers* on *earth*

Inhabitants, in the Hebrew, simply mean people who have lived in a place a long time. It has the idea of sitting down to stay. They are not planning to go anywhere. The word *world* means firm, dry land, soil. It does not have the nuance of meaning found in the New Testament that the world is symbolic for what is wrong in God's order of things. Here it is where vegetation would grow. Thus, they are people all over the world who consider Earth their permanent home. The Bible has some things to say to them:

- In Psalm 33:8 they are told they should stand in awe of God.
- In Psalm 49:1 they are instructed that compared to God, man is inadequate.
- In Isaiah 18:3 (our verse) they are to witness God's judgment.
- In Isaiah 26:9 through God's judgment they are to learn righteousness.

- In Isaiah 26:18 they are not born again, but are not wicked (26:10)
- In Isaiah 38:11 Hezekiah laments his premature death will prevent him from seeing them.
- Lamentations 4:12 says neither kings nor they will believe God will bring judgment on Jerusalem and it will fall.

Dwellers in the Hebrew means to settle, reside, tabernacle or be enthroned (God). It does not carry the connotation of permanence. They are not tied to the place, as are the inhabitants, above. *Earth* means the same as world, but with the caveat of a particular people living in a certain place, like a country. Usually, in the Old Testament, it refers to a specific parcel of land; Israel. The word is *eres* in Hebrew. It does not convey the idea of supporting vegetation. Combine these two meanings and one has the suggestion of Christians who are alive, living in the Kingdom of God, awaiting the rapture.

What we end up with in this remarkable verse two groups of people are addressed on planet Earth at the time of the attack on America: believers and a specific group of non-believers. The believers are the dwellers. They have no permanence here. Nor, does their life require labor in order to sustain it. This idea is coming from the lack of soil in the meaning. It is connected to Adam's curse of having to labor the soil in order to survive. As they are living life as a follower of Jesus, their life does not require labor, i.e., the sense that the individual has to make things happen, to work things out, to struggle with decisions. It is a life lived by faith. Faith in being protected, directed along the correct path, having verve, vitality, joy and the assurance one is eternally part of God's family. It is living daily with God's priceless present, as Chuck Swindoll, currently the pastor of Stonebriar Community Church in Frisco, Texas describes Romans 8:28, and we know that God causes all things to work together for good to those who love God, to those who are called according to His purpose. Now, since both groups are still on the earth, the rapture has not yet occurred. That fact, in itself, begs the question, why would God have Isaiah separately point them out? The answer is two-fold. The first is alluded to in Isaiah 26:9, 10. The inhabitants of the world learn righteousness from the judgment; the wicked do not. Thus, God does not bother to address them, because their hearts are hardened and they themselves are the targets of the judgment. They inhabitants of the world are the remnant of humans who live through the Tribulation and go into the millennium. The second is to call attention to the Christians. Both groups are present, yet they are not mentioned again in this verse and the dwellers on the earth are not mentioned again in the bible.

No reference to these two groups of people is made to any other nation Isaiah addresses in the woe chapters. Beyond the major message I referred to in the preceding paragraph, I believe another reason is that most of the inhabitants of this nation think of themselves as Christians when asked their religious affiliation, though disturbing trends are taking place. People are falling away from the faith. Yet, Jesus' warning in Revelation Chapter Three to the Laodicea church, I fear applies to many. They have no commitment to what they profess to believe. Jesus describes them as lukewarm. In fact, as in the Song of Solomon, they are spiritually asleep; oblivious to the times in which they are living. Remember the story? The bridegroom comes to her door and knocks. The meaning in Hebrew is to beat with the fist. His love, the church, is asleep. I am not including in this count the millions of Americans, who think say they are Christians when asked, but have no understanding or commitment to salvation, being born again or of the atonement and most importantly, have no personal relationship with Jesus. He says clearly in Matthew 7:23, "...I never knew you, depart from me..." Then again in Matthew 26:12 he answered the five foolish virgins, "Truly I say to you, I never knew you." Of everything concerning Christianity after the Cross, this is preeminent: a personal relationship with Jesus. The Barna Group, a company who does survey's and interprets the state

Chapter Four: The Bad News

of the country's beliefs, published that only 8% of those claiming Christianity as their faith believed Jesus was the Son of God and he was the only way to salvation through the acceptance of his blood, via his sacrificial death, as substitute for their own deserved eternal separation from God. This is a clarion call to all of us who do understand the fundamentals of the Faith to get busy and evangelize. Time is so, so short.

At the first of this chapter we talked about how commanders signaled their armies to commence a battle. The standard was raised on the mountain or hill (the same Hebrew word can mean both). Here, the standard is raised in several mountains. So, do we have a coordinated, simultaneous attack? I think we do. It is one signal (raised flag) to initiate several simultaneous attacks. It is interesting to me most of the world's population is watching when this command is given and hearing the sound of the trumpet call to battle. Is this to be taken literally? Will the world's population be watching when whatever happens to trigger the judgment? Do the mountains represent governments of some form who respond to the command? Or, is this a multifaceted event triggering a natural disaster? I just find it most curious that mountain is plural and the world is already watching because on 9/11 the world did not really begin to tune in until after the first plane hit the World Trade Center and the second hit the Pentagon. Apparently, the audience is already in place for this. Even so, I am going to step out into the heavy mist of speculation and offer a possibility, but I need to get more of Isaiah's vision in context.

A summary now of Isaiah's warning may be helpful. In the first two verses, Isaiah identified the nation by a marker of direction from a point he knew. He described the most salient things about the nation: geography, description of the people physically and politically and he told about activities causing this woe to come upon them. This verse alerts the world to the judgment's start. In Verse Four, coming up, a big change is to take place.

Verses 4

For thus the LORD has told me, I will look from [in] My dwelling place quietly like dazzling heat in the sunshine, like a cloud of dew in the heat of harvest.[33]

I wish to add a technical note about this verse. And, it applies to most translations. It is called for because of the addition of word *in* which I added to the text. Occasionally, translators will change a word (usually annotated) or add a word (usually italics) both of which are to clarify the meaning. Beyond that, Hebrew has about 10,000 words. Greek has 100,000. Many words in Hebrew get the

Chapter Four: The Bad News

nuance of their meaning from within the context in which they are used. In my opinion, they missed it here, because their paradigm was Cush, not a nation yet to exist. The translated text says He will look *from* His dwelling place. If He were to have looked *out* from His dwelling place (the spiritual realm we call Heaven), He would have seen events taking place in our realm. By looking *in* He sees what has not yet happened in our realm, as most of the Book of Revelation has not yet happened. He is thus seeing what is going to happen and explaining it to Isaiah. Why is that important? Certainly, that is a fair question. When we think of God's judgments in the Old Testament, we think of His use of other countries using force or allowing natural disasters. An example of the use of force would be the Babylonian captivity. A natural disaster would be the destruction of Sodom and Gomorra. In this whole chapter Isaiah has been telling us of a vision he saw and the message he understood the vision to mean. Now it changes. God is now telling Isaiah what He wants him to say. God is no longer showing; now, He is telling. It is as though He wants Isaiah to be very precise, not interpretive.

The next word *dazzling* is used many times in scripture to characterize the way angels appear or the way Jesus does in His incarnate state. This dazzling is so bright the human eye can barely look at it. It can also represent God in action in our realm and in that sense it is like the word glory. The Bible makes the direct statement: ...God is Light, and in Him there is no darkness at all. [34] From Genesis 1:2, God spoke light into the world and it was good. [35] What it means, besides creating the physical light and its benefits, is that God's spiritual presence came into the spiritual darkness and separated the two. In doing so, a place was defined to confine the spiritual darkness, where chaos, confusion and purposelessness are present. Here, however, I suggest it does not have that beneficial purpose. Remember, this is God removing completely His increase of good (blessing). Whatever it is seems to be in a flash of light so brilliant the human eye cannot easily view it, if the eye can even stand to see it. The next word is *heat*.

Heat appears here and in the next clause. *Heat* had two main metaphorical meanings to the Jews. First, it was a punishment for disobedience. Second, relief from heat would come in the promised restoration of Israel. We are not Israel. This blinding flash of light is connected with heat; the meaning is literal, not metaphorical.

The dazzling heat appears as it does in bright sunshine. The image I have is that of a hot, summer afternoon sun burning down on pavement. The air near the pavement is heated, breaking the light rays and rising up from the surface into the less hot air above. It seems to shimmer. Movie makers use this footage to convey the hot

Chapter Four: The Bad News

temperature in a scene. Only here, I sense, the scale is much larger. It will be an event so dramatic peoples of the world, including those in the unnamed nation, watch it. While, perhaps, as experts expounded theories of what is about to happen and the effects.

The next clause reads: *like a cloud of dew in the heat of harvest*. Jennifer Meyers, meteorologist for KDFW Fox 4 television in Dallas, Texas tells me there is no meteorological term for cloud of dew; it is an ancient description of fog. The presence of clouds in scripture generally represents God's presence; albeit, as fearful as they are, they are more passive than seeing Him as light. So the implication is that God is behind the dew, or fog, in the heat of harvest. Dew, and rain, throughout the Tanakh (complete Old Testament) represent blessing. In the growing season dew is very heavy in Israel and is sufficient to supply moisture for growth to the plant – thus, the blessing (increase). In this case, this action of what is normally God's blessing takes place in the heat of harvest. But during the harvest, the plant is already grown. Now, dew is more of a hindrance than blessing. Yet, it comes as a fog, thereby signifying abundance, a complete covering. Whatever the event is, it will be everywhere.

How then, does this event tie into the heat of harvest? Ancient rabbinic tradition had the idea of the harvest was a foreshadowing of

God harvesting their souls. So, when Jesus spoke of the people coming out of Samara in the story at Jacob's Well in John Four (the woman at the well), his disciples knew exactly the implication when He said that the fields are white for harvest: this was how the harvesting of souls was to take place: the righteous, in white robes, would come out of the sin–soaked world, symbolized by the city.

Let us amplify Verse Four in the light of understanding the depth of the meaning of its words. I call to your mind Proverbs 25:2: *It is the glory of God to conceal a matter, but the glory of kings is to search out a matter.* In the spirit of Proverbs, I render the meaning of the verse this way. God speaks directly to Isaiah and tells him, "This is what I see happening at My direction. It will be taking place concerning the unnamed nation. With some advanced warning, an event(s) will take place. My angels will cause the people of the world to see brilliant light. Heat will be connected to the light. The heat is so intense its presence will also be visible; people will see shimmering."

> *For thus the Lord has told me, I will look from [in] my dwelling place quietly like dazzling heat in the sunshine, like a cloud of dew in the heat of harvest.*
> Isaiah 18: 4

Our interest in the timing of prophecies is almost as strong an allure for us as future event itself. When will it happen is almost

Chapter Four: The Bad News

always the second question. I don't know what year the event will happen. Let me repeat, I do not know. God has not revealed it to me. What follows is my own personal opinion.

There is an interesting clue, however, as it appears to take place in conjunction with other prophetic events. We have already discussed the woe chapters; the judgment of the nations. It would seem these judgments take place prior to the famous Battle of Armageddon. Ezekiel 34:4-6 lists the nations who will come against Israel in the final, climatic battle. The woe nations are not among them and for the most part, they are the nations currently surrounding Israel or in close proximity, except for the United States. So what happened to them? These are the nations listed in Palm 83, which describes the threatening challenge to Israel in the Middle East of today. It can only mean one of two things. Either these nations no longer exist as they do now and have no fighters to field in battle. Or, if they do exist, their relationship with Israel is no longer that of aggressor nations. In this age, our age, the latter seems farfetched, indeed.

Of all the nations God judges for the way they treated Israel, only Moab (today's Jordan), Egypt, a part of the nations on the Arabian Peninsula, Tyre (today's Lebanon) and the unnamed nation are said to have a remnant remaining. Of those, only the unnamed nation is noted for sending a delegation to Jerusalem to bring a gift and pay homage to the King. This tells me the others may already be incorporated into Israel as all of them now live in part of the land God promised Abraham and his seed. To be clear, I think the judgment of the nations is in the timeframe connected to or a part of the Great Tribulation. The people in these nations, remnant to be, who were not killed in the woe judgment, have to endure the second one, the Day of Judgment. After the Battle of Armageddon, when Jesus takes the thrown as King of Kings these people are no longer citizens of their former nation, rather citizens of Israel. The American remnant, on the other hand, does go into the millennium as a nation.

Our national prayer, in light of this, should be, "Dear God, please have mercy in your judgment on us." The time for God to bless America has vanished with the wind of unheeded warnings because of our disregard for His covenant with Israel — the focus of His eye.

Verses 5

For before the harvest, as soon as the bud blossoms and the flower becomes a ripening grape, then He will cut off the sprigs with pruning knives and remove and cut away the spreading branches. [36]

Now, Isaiah resumes his recount of the vision for us, following God's interruption. So, when and what does Isaiah see now?

Chapter Four: The Bad News

Timing of the event occurs before the harvest which takes place in September/October. Timing of the bud to blossom, which in the Hebrew actually means the blossom has finished and the grape appears is the May time period. The beginning of ripening, known as the stage of veraison, starts about the end of July or early August. In this July/August timeframe one would expect the event to occur. The problem is that is not what the text says. Isaiah is not referring to what God told him in Verse Three, he has resumed his vision. The word then does not refer to a time after, it refers to when the period occurs, i.e., after the grape is ripening, but before the harvest. It says in this timeframe He will begin to cut off sprigs and remove spreading branches. We will deal with what this means momentarily, but let's be clear on the timing of Verse Four, the commencement of the event(s) that God told Isaiah and Verse Five, the timing of the cutting off of the sprigs and removal of the branches.

Remember our discussion in Chapter Three concerning how the period of Israel's judgment was calculated? God does not act randomly. This judgment is not one He takes lightly. The day it comes will be a day of significance both to God and the country itself. What might be to most probable choices? Nowhere does Isaiah say the two events occur consecutively in the same timeframe. Nor, does he say they don't. But think about it logically. If He is going to use a military invasion of the country, how is that going to be so obvious to the inhabitants of the world and dwellers of the earth? By the same token, how will they see the attack order given? No military commander would announce to the world his command to commence battle while announcing it to his troops simultaneously. It violates the element of surprise. I think this is a natural phenomenon God orchestrates which rivets the world's attention in shock and awe. Following this, sometime later, the terrorists come and then even later, the invasion forces.

We are all now on the same page of understanding, so let us return to what Isaiah is telling us. The sprigs on a grape vine Isaiah speaks about produce no fruit; the fruit of grapes is produced on established branches. Small grapes and small clusters grow out toward the end of the branch whose end becomes a sprig after the harvest, no longer able to produce. Isaiah tells us they are cut off by Him (God). Non-producing vegetation is a recurring same metaphor for so called Christians who produce no fruit. One is the Parable of the Wheat and Tares. Tares look like wheat when

> *For before the harvest, as soon as the bud blossoms and the flower becomes a ripening grape, then He will cut off the sprigs with pruning knives and remove and cut away the spreading branches.*
>
> Isaiah 18: 5

Chapter Four: The Bad News

maturing, but fail to produce the kernel that will become fruit. At the end of the age, the two are separated by angels; tares for destruction, the wheat (Christians) taken into the barn (safety) to wait thrashing (the rapture — separation from the body). Isaiah also mentioned spreading branches.

Spreading branches on a grape vine are the lowest branches and then others, higher up, who just never produce. I'll deal with the lowest ones in the next paragraph, but now I want to concentrate on these higher spreading branches. Though they are watered and get sunlight, they are worthless because all they do is sap energy from the trunk the producing branches could use. These lives offer no redeeming surrender to God, but they masquerade as a part of the Vine.

Jesus teaches a lesson about the three sizes of grapes a vine produces after his last Seder (we know it as the Last Supper) on his way to Gethsemane. It is a teaching showing us the three levels of Christian maturity. John the Apostle was listening, because he expands on this measure of spiritual growth in his first letter. It is the last lesson Jesus teaches his disciples and is found in John 15:1, 6. The late Dr. Bruce Wilkinson, along with David Kopp, penned a most informative teaching about this story in their book, *The Secrets of the Vine*.[37] The spreading branches to which they refer grow close to the ground and get little sunlight. During rain, they will typically be bent down and the leaves fall into the ground's mud. What sunlight does get through can't penetrate the mud sufficiently so grapes don't grow. The vinedresser, God, lifts them up, washes off the mud and ties them up so they can begin to produce. They are not damned as someone reading without understanding might conclude. Isaiah's focus is on the ones who are higher and do not produce.

Isaiah 18 — When

Amos 3:7 tells us that surely the Lord GOD does nothing unless He reveals His secret counsel to His servants the prophets. Again, this verse has no hidden secrets to reveal. God will not do anything that will affect you without making it known to you in advance. He has given us enough clues to know time of the year these two events will happen. He has not told us what year. We may never know the year in advance with certainty, but we surely will know the season of years.

The season of this judgment is first of all determined from world events. The case has been made that America has crossed from warning to judgment by virtue of our stubborn rebellion to God's repeated warnings. Second, He places warnings for people on earth in the heavens. This is amazing to me and I think it will be to you.

Chapter Four: The Bad News

Genesis One contains the blueprint for how things are to work between the natural and spiritual realms. It is a remarkable chapter. This is how it reads concerning the purpose of what was created on the fourth day in Genesis 1:14. Then God said, "Let there be lights in the expanse of the heavens to separate the day from the night, and let them be for signs and for seasons and for days and years; and let them be for lights in the expanse of the heavens to give light on the earth; and it was so." [38] Thus, the purpose of the sun and moon is to:

> *For before the harvest, as soon as the bud blossoms and the flower becomes a ripening grape, then He will cut off the sprigs with pruning knives and remove and cut away the spreading branches.*
> Isaiah 18: 5

1. Be in charge of separating the light and darkness on earth just as God separated them spiritually in Genesis 1:4.

2. Act as signs from God to people on earth.

3. Regulate the seasons, which are not spring, summer, fall and winter, rather God's appointed times (*moed in Hebrew*); we know them as His feasts.

4. Be a counting means so people can account for time, not only as to days, but years, as well (lunar and solar).

What I want us to focus on is that of the second most important purpose, above, to send signs or signals to the earth! The accounting for time on the clock and calendar are last. Throughout history, man has connected surprising events in the heavens with events on the earth. Man has not always lived in this fast—paced world. It was just over one hundred years ago we could not travel faster than a horse. Until the telegraph, the spread of information was limited to a man's speed of travel. Celestial events such as comets visible with the naked eye, solar and lunar eclipses, especially total ones, do not occur often. They were frightening and foreboding to this planet's inhabitants. As a result, when destruction would later fall in the close proximity of time, they connected it to the previous celestial event. A clear pattern immerged over time. A total solar eclipse meant a warning of coming sorrows to a nation or nations other than Israel. Total lunar eclipses meant the same for Israel. It was God speaking then, just as He is speaking now.

Up until now, His warnings to America, as we have seen, have been in the form of natural disasters and enemy attacks. Those were warnings. The celestial activities warn of judgment. If I am correct that the judgment of nations is timed close to or with the Great Tribulation, then celestially, they will receive the same warning. Now, here comes one amazing warning.

On July 16, 1994, the Shoemaker—Levy Comet began to impact the surface of Jupiter. It was the first celestial collision ever

Chapter Four: The Bad News

witnessed by man. Astronomers witnessed twenty—one visible impacts hit the surface of the planet. The last to be visibly witnessed was on July 22, 1994. [39] For seven days the show fulfilled the dreams of many of these astronomers. July 22, 1994 was on a Saturday, the day of the week the Jewish Sabbath is celebrated. It was 8 Av 5774 on the calendar the Jews observe. The next day, Sunday, is the Ninth of Av. A day remembered annually with fasting by the Jews for on this day, the children of the exodus refused to cross the Jordan and enter the Promised Land, both Temples were destroyed, in 133 A.D., the final Jewish revolt against Rome occurred and the Temple Mount was plowed under followed by the beginning of the Great Diaspora, Jews were kicked out of England in 1290, and in 1492 the last Jew was expelled from Spain. For this celestial event to have been witnessed from earth in connection with a Jewish Sabbath, happening over the Ninth of Av and lasting seven days (key biblical number) it has to be God speaking. The crowning surety to this is that the Sabbath's word that day in Jewish worship services was *devarim*. This word means to say words that have a message to convey. God had something very important to say to the world through the Shoemaker—Levy Comet and to the most important nation in the world.

Seven years later, in the United States, 9/11 occurs on a Tuesday. On the following Monday, the Stock Market crashes and the next day the country's economy loses seven percent of its value. This Monday, on the Jewish calendar is 29 Elul, the last day of the Jewish civil year.

More digression is required here, but it is important we are on the same page. Remember back to the phenomenal prophecy by Ezekiel which was connected to the punishment placed on the nation of Israel for not observing the Shmitah years. (This is the year when debts were to be settled and the land was to have its rest.) Well, 2000—2001 was a Shmitah year and on September 17th, the 29th of Elul (the last day of the Shmitah year) the market crashed. The next Shmitah came in 2008. The Stock Market severely dipped again. The economy lost seven percent. The date the market crashed was the Monday, the 29th; both of September and Elul. The economy of the world almost followed, but recovered. The next Shmitah will be in 2015; this Shmitah may prove much worse for the United States and the world. The 29th of Elul will be September 13th. The pattern would indicate another seven percent drop in the economy. I believe it will be much, much worse. I think America's heralded financial collapse comes on 29 Elul, September 13, 2015. That is not the event

Chapter Four: The Bad News

of Isaiah's focus, but it will make for a very weak America; worse than the Great Depression of the 1930's.

The reason I predict this collapse goes back to the Shoemaker—Levy Comet's impact on Jupiter. It took twenty—one days, three sets of seven, for men of earth to witness the impacts. This will be the third Shmitah year and the last of the three seven day counts ending with Shoemaker—Levy. Remember Super Storm Sandy and compare that event to the others in severity. She, too, was the last one in the cycle of warning. That does not mean the connected disasters to the land for peace initiatives will now cease. The judgment has been declared. Comparing this to our legal system, we are now in the sentencing phase where we can repent and plead for mercy. I am convinced God does not want to do this to us, but He must because of the covenant. Again, if you are thinking that none of these Jewish days applies to America, remember, they are not Jewish; they are God's. It is just the Jews are the only people who observe them. The hidden secret revealed by the Number Three continues.

The end of the three sevens will also be witness to the eighth tetrad since the first coming of Jesus. Before I get to the tetrad, I need to make a comment about the number eight. Biblically, it is the number signifying divine completion and a new beginning. A tetrad is when there are four complete lunar eclipses in consecutive order.

The implication of these tetrads of 2014/2015 is fascinating, as many evangelical Christians believe they are the final harbingers of the last days. What Christian cannot have both apprehension and excitement when they realize God has chosen them to live in the end of the age; the waning moments of the Day of Grace? The reason I used the word *fascinating* for these tetrads and presumed to speak what Christians feel in response is because they occur on Jewish holidays. Solar eclipses also occur. Much has been written and spoken about what significance both might portend. For our purposes, what these tetrads mean to Isaiah's prophecy is that we are at the completion of the age. So, in spite of the accelerated turmoil coming in the Middle East, we need to stay focused on Isaiah's unnamed nation and when judgment falls on America.

> *For before the harvest, as soon as the bud blossoms and the flower becomes a ripening grape, then He will cut off the sprigs with pruning knives and remove and cut away the spreading branches.*
> Isaiah 18: 5

Remember that Isaiah saw early in his vision emissaries traveling across the ocean. These are American diplomats traveling to the Middle East to forge land for peace. Since these trips represent America's policy challenging God's covenant, I thought it a good

Chapter Four: The Bad News

place to check when it started. I am convinced now, as I was then, the day this happens will not be an arbitrary day on our calendar, but a day of significance to God.

Prior to the Madrid Peace Conference of 1991, I can't find any record of our shuttle diplomacy being focused on a Palestinian state forged out of covenant land. Do not get me wrong. They were all focused on peace in the region, just not this vehicle as a solution. A Palestinian state was suggested by the UN in 1947; the Palestinians refused. They have always refused because they don't want a state next to Israel; they want Israel without Jews. Following the Madrid Conference in October, 1991, a follow-up conference was held in Moscow on January 28 — 29, 1992. Land for peace was not on the agenda.

I felt I was staring at the proverbial brick wall. (I want to share how it evolved for those of you who too are struggling to hear something from God. Maybe this will be of some help.) My spirit, on the other hand, kept hearing, "Look at the Madrid Conference." I have two television shows I watch, including reruns of them. It isn't the plot nearly as much as the quality of acting and the script the writers give the characters. These two are *NCIS* and *Castle*, particularly *Castle*. A few nights before, we had watched a *Castle* rerun. The key to the plot was a brilliant mind who could find a lynchpin event which would cause other events to happen much like dominoes fall when properly spaced and the first one is toppled. I remembered the word *lynchpin*. (I didn't hear it on my own; the Holy Spirit recalled it for me at the proper time.) So, I looked for the lynchpin event, connected to the Madrid Conference in time, which would have permitted land for peace to gain a foothold. I found it and it fit perfectly. That Peace I was so desperately seeking came over me and I knew God had given me the answer. Here it is.

Leading up to the Madrid Conference, the Bush Administration had a hard time getting the Israeli government of Prime Minister Shamir to attend. Shamir had asked for a $10 million dollar loan for transporting Russian Jews to Israel and settling them. The Bush administration linked this to Israel's attendance in Madrid and cessation of settlement expansion. Shamir called Bush's bluff, but Bush held. Shamir gave in and came. Throughout the process Shamir never acceded to stop building settlements in territory acquired in the 1967 War, a consistent request of the Bush Administration and an added condition for the loan following Madrid. Shamir's government did, however, fall out of favor because of Madrid and the Likud government came to power in June 22, 1992. On July 19, the parliament passed a resolution partially halting settlement construction. Israel subsequently was granted the loan in August. The lynchpin was the

Chapter Four: The Bad News

vote on July 19th. It opened the door to the idea that Israel could be coerced to give up land.

July 19, 1992 on the Gregorian calendar was the 18 of Tammuz on the solar/lunar calendar. The day before, on the 17th and centuries before, Moses broke the stone tablets containing the Ten Commandments when he witnessed worship of the Golden Calf, as he came off the mountain. This date has other significance in Jewish history, but I want us to focus on Moses. The nest day, Moses destroyed the calf, mixed its dust with water and had the people drink of it. The following morning, those who had worshipped the Calf mysteriously died from an enlarged stomach, while those who had not worshipped were not sick. The not so subtle point I am making is those who acted wrongly brought death to themselves through the same agency. It is a consistent theme throughout scripture, when the rule is violated, the prime mover in its violation is the agent of chastening; an eye for an eye. If you gain by violence; by violence you are brought down. (Proverbs 1:19, et al). Understand I am not talking about covenant here. We have squeezed Israel to give up land which, in this day, provides her a limited warning. In so doing we would make her defenseless. The judgment on us will make us defenseless. It will happen on the 18th of Tammuz (about mid-July), after the grapes have begun to ripen, but before the harvest. What year will this be?

If I am correct about the coming Shmitah being the collapse of our economy, 2016/2017 would be likely candidates. As a nation, the United States will be very vulnerable to any attack when we can't pay for things we need on the international market. Certainly we can barter assets, but how for does that go? By the summer of 2016 or 2017, we would be in just such a vulnerable position. Society would have begun to collapse. Inflation would be rampant, government checks would be worthless and nationally, our assets would be exhausted. Plans of our adversaries would be well under way to proselyte, pillage and plunder.

Isaiah 18 — How

Now, this is the scenario that I think is most likely to happen. A solar storm erupts on the sun it is more powerful than others. So powerful it captures the attention of the scientific community immediately and thus, the media who follow them. It makes for good video and a good crisis, so it begins to be covered by the networks with their legion of experts. The worldwide media picks it up and soon, the whole world is watching. As the fires shoot out from the surface, the long range camera lens through the atmosphere makes the solar storms off the sun's surface appear to shimmer. The sunspots dazzle.

Chapter Four: The Bad News

A cluster of flares send out a solar storm of magnetic waves toward the spot in space where the earth will be as they cross the plane of our orbit. The United States is facing the sun at this moment, so we absorb a direct hit. The effect is an EMP or electromagnetic pulse. It fits the description God gave Isaiah perfectly. Born of light and heat, its effect is like that of a cloud of dew; no noise and completely covering an area. In this case, it will cover most or all of the contiguous 48 states. Should you not be aware of the effect of an EMP, let me enlighten you with some information I recently learned.

My primary source of this information is from an engineering friend of mine, John D. Mitchell, who first alerted me to what this is and, subsequently, F. Michael Maloof through his book, *A Nation Forsaken, EMP: The Escalating Threat of an American Catastrophe*.[40] For decades, Mr. Maloof has been warning of this impending disaster, al beit, unknown to me. He has been ignored by our government and industry to provide protection for the public. The military and parts of the government have been protected. I cannot urge you in terms strong enough to read his book. The book is available through WND, Amazon, Barnes and Noble and many other bookseller outlets. If all you learn of an EMP is from the following paragraph, then you are doing yourself and your family a huge disservice.

An EMP can be caused by a nuclear explosion, a solar flare, or on a much smaller scale a radio frequency (RF) weapon. Parts to construct an RF weapon may be purchased at Radio Shack. In order to affect all of America, a nuclear explosion would have to detonate 200 miles above the center of the country. North Korea, intelligence reports, is working on delivering just such a weapon. The damaging solar flares from the sun strike the earth on average every 100 years. So, why you may ask, have we not been damaged before? It is because we did not have solid state circuitry. Without a shield, an EMP striking solid state circuitry will render it totally impotent; otherwise, it has no adverse effect on us or the planet. In today's America, everything runs on solid state circuitry. Everything without a shield, that needs a fuel source to operate, will become inoperable in less than a second. An EMP would knock out all electricity. Our electric grid is managed by nodes which are controlled by unshielded solid state circuitry. Anything running on electricity no longer will work, including automobile engines built after 1972, regardless of its fuel source. Engines who are 30,000 feet in altitude when the EMP hits and the ones under hoods will immediately stop. In the blink of an eye, America will revert to the 17th Century, without the supporting infrastructure. And, we can't just fix it. The machines to manufacture and repair won't work either. Our nighttime light

Chapter Four: The Bad News

and heat will come from candles and fires. There will be no air conditioning, no running water in homes. We can travel no faster than a horse. Within days, the country will be in a state of anarchy. It will take a very long time to recover from this and before we can, the nation will be extremely vulnerable to attack from terrorists and other nations. The survivalists who are storing food and water can't store enough. The only people who have a hope of surviving are those on a farm with firewood, cows, chickens, a well and the ability to grow crops and can food. The rest of us are at the mercy of God. This is His judgment and only God can get a person through it. Those persons will be the future remnant and those in relationship with Jesus. If I have said this before, or if I repeat myself, please pardon me, but this is so important it bears repeating. A relationship is forged when people talk to one another, communicating information about themselves, over time. Read your Bible, God is talking to you through it. Find a quiet place and talk to Jesus as though he were sitting next to you. Listen for His voice inside you. Learn to bind the Devil from putting thoughts in your mind so that you can depend on what you are thinking is from God. The 19th of Tammuz is too late.

Having said all of the above, let me say again, I do not know for certain when or what is going to happen any more than we know for certain we are going to wake up in the morning. I am certain the things described in Verse Four, are going to happen. After they happen, Isaiah tells us of the aftermath.

Verse 6

They will be left together for mountain birds of prey and for the beasts of the earth; and the birds of prey will spend the summer feeding on them, and all the beasts of the earth will spend harvest time on them. [41]

Verse Three left us with the attack on America broadcast to the entire world. We had the flashback in verses four and five. Now, verse six picks up from verse three to continue telling what happens on the timeline.

The word starting the verse is *they*, referring back to the sprigs and spreading branches. Let me first say who they are not. They are not the inhabitants of the world (those reserved to be the remnant) and the dwellers on the earth (born again Christians). Having identified who they are not, I think we can safely assume who they are; people who produce no spiritual fruit in their lives because they have no relationship with Jesus. These are people we all know who do not give a thought to Jesus. They are out from under God's protection entirely. They are people who have wickedness in their heart. When

Chapter Four: The Bad News

the event happens and its aftermath, they will have to endure what comes without hope; lambs to the slaughter, so to speak.

Those who think they are Christians, but without a relationship and with a wicked heart, are cut away from the vine. They are not left to lie on the ground in a literal sense. Rather, they are gathered as the vine dresser would pick them up just as the tares were in Jesus' parable, they are bundled and reserved for the fire. These, of course, are all metaphorical pictures of what will actually happen. They won't physically go anywhere. I think the best way to explain this is with another picture. Think back with me to the story beginning in Genesis Ten of the first Passover. In that story, the blood of the sacrificial lamb was spread on the door posts, the lintel and the transom. (In doing so, it formed the points of the cross Jesus's blood was to stain.) Because the mark of blood was on the entrance to that house, the Angel of Death passes over it. The houses he entered had no mark. So it is here. Without a mark of protection, they are left behind for the mountain birds and beasts. These are the tares.

The wheat has gone into the barn — a place of protection. The promise is of protection from what is to come. One may well ask if this refers to the rapture. I do not think it does. I think the rapture comes on a Rosh Hashanah, God's Feast of Trumpets. But this is a good time to point out why the future is not clear prophetically.

The reason we don't know the timing of certain coming prophetic events is this: if God told us, the enemy would overhear and know. He gives us signs it is soon, but not always when. The result is that we get muddled teaching on end time events. I am convinced things will happen that will be a surprise, both to us and the adversary.

First come the *mountain birds of prey*, Isaiah tells us. So, what can we deduce from the description? An eagle, falcon or hawk is a mountain bird of prey. They have keen eyesight, scout out their prey and descend without warning to strike. What human entity comes to mind correlating to this type behavior? Let's approach it differently.

The word *mountain* (and sometimes hill) in scripture, especially prophetic scriptures, almost always refers to a kingdom, government, or ruler over a particular people. These birds then would be some type of agents of one of the world's mountains. The agents' mission would be that of killing. I have a very strong speculation as to who these birds of prey are, but it is going to take some explaining. How are you not surprised?

The Book of Daniel tells us of four kingdoms, or empires, beginning with the one holding Daniel captive. All of these, we are told, come from Israel's north to menace. In scripture, Israel's enemies almost always come from the North. The menorah, in the Holy Place, representing God's revelation of Himself, is against the

Chapter Four: The Bad News

North wall. It is God who reveals these enemies to Daniel. They are not named, but Daniel gives enough clues that history has identified three. They are Babylonians, followed by the Medes-Persians, followed by the Greeks. The fourth beast is assumed by many to be the return of the Romans, yet to reappear on the world's stage as the Revived Roman Empire. I respectfully disagree. Now, this is one of those "button issues."

A button issue is when somebody says something contrary to a closely held belief or understanding of another person. The new contrary statement pushes their button of rejection. Because it was said or, in this case written, that person cannot be right — on anything. It goes like this: if they cannot be right on this most important, fundamental point (again, in the person's estimation), then everything else they say is wrong and they hit the eject button. Please don't, at least not until you finish reading the explanation. Then, ask the Spirit within you to confirm this with God's peace.

One reason I disagree is because Daniel tells us this kingdom is unlike any other. That does not fit the Roman Empire, because it was just like the other three. They were all political entities. Second, Rome never ruled from Babylon. The closest they got was 70 miles. Third, this fourth kingdom has the two legs of Daniel's image. This does fit the divided Roman Empire, but only for a few short years. A few years after the Eastern capital was moved to Istanbul in 1299, the Western capital, Rome, fell to the Barbarians in 1453. For only 154 years then was Rome a divided kingdom. The Empire that did rule the geography covering the territory ruled by the Babylonians, Medes-Persians and Greeks was the Islamic caliphate of the Ottoman Empire. And yes, they ruled the lands of the Assyrians and Roman Empire, as well. They ruled the land of Israel. Like none of the others, including Rome, they left a testament of their presence in the form of their religion: Islam. They were not only a political entity, but a religious one as well. They were like no other kingdom. The two legs of Daniel's image supporting Islam are the Shiites and Sunnis. World War I witnessed the final exit of the Ottomans after over a century of rule from the stage of history, but the dreams of the caliphate live on in the hearts of Muslims.

> *They will be left together for mountain birds of prey and for the beasts of the earth; and the birds of prey will spend the summer feeding on them, and all the beasts of the earth will spend harvest time on them.*
> Isaiah 18:6

What made the Ottomans like no other kingdom is the Islamic caliphate. It was a military power. It was a ruling authority under Shariah Law. Even though there were separate kingdoms within, their commonality was Islam. Under this central authority they

Chapter Four: The Bad News

united then, as I believe they will again. The revival of the caliphate and the empire's rebirth will come when one much anticipated figure takes the stage of history. He is the Mahdi, the redeemer of Islam who, according to Islamic eschatology, appears just before Judgment Day. Today, Islam is spreading very fast around the globe. The fourth kingdom of Daniel's image is about to be resurrected. And, its most well know agents are already on stage. We know them as militant Islamic terrorists.

In Rabbi Jonathan Cahn's narration of the WND movie *The Isaiah 9:10 Judgment*, he explains the Assyrians breached the wall of Jerusalem in 701 B.C. and were driven back. Twenty years later they returned; this time to capture the city Samara and lay siege to Jerusalem. Assyria was the first empire to employ terrorism against adversaries. Terrorists from the same geographical area breached America's wall (the Atlantic Ocean) in 2001. I do believe the same will be back as mountain birds of prey.

The Bible gives a reinforcing clue in Jeremiah 12:8a. Here is the quote: "Is My inheritance like a speckled bird of prey to Me? Are the birds of prey against her on every side?" God is speaking, of course. His inheritance is Israel and a speckled bird is one who would draw the attention of other birds. The clue comes next. Who surrounds

Israel today on every side and picks at her people as a bird would? Is it not Islamic terrorists? They are the mountain birds of prey.

Their mission will be to convert everyone to Islam. Those who do convert will be akin to indentured servants. Those who don't will be killed. Many will die from the indiscriminate bombings we are so familiar with from watching the Middle East. As a nation, we will drink from the same cup Israel has drunk, but on a much larger scale. After a time, the *feeding* of the birds of prey will be finished followed by beasts of the earth. It doesn't get any better with them being here.

Beasts represent nations who behave like wild animals in the way they execute conquests of other nations. The kingdoms of Daniel are also described as beasts. The type of beast for who they are named is the way that beast would attack its prey. Isaiah tells us that America will be invaded by a group of nations who behave like ravenous animals toward us. How many will there be, we do not know, but I would guess four because that is how many Israel endured. How much of the country will they conquer, we don't know. We do know life for those who are left, will be no better than it was under the birds of prey — the terrorists. How long this terror and the following invasions take place is told us by Isaiah.

He says the birds of prey will spend the summer *feeding* on our people and the invading nations will spend all of harvest time. A quick aside on when summer occurs is in order. There is a meteorological timing for summer and an astronomical one. Meteorological has to do with the timing variations from year to year of the shifts in climate. While astronomical has a fixed time in the relationship to the earth and sun. In the First Century, only the astronomical system was used. Here are the dates: spring began on our March 20, summer on June 21, fall on September 21, and winter on December 21. Literal interpretation would tell one that by winter it will all be over. I do not think that is the case. The reference of time Isaiah gave us as to the time of the grapes ripening is not, I believe, continuing on the same timeline as what is happening in Verse Six. The reason, I submit, is the way verse seven begins: At that time, a gift of homage will be brought to the Lord of hosts...even Mount Zion. This clearly refers to Jesus sitting on His thrown in Jerusalem, after Armageddon and the Tribulation are over. The tribulation timeframe has to figure in for all or more of this time of birds of prey and beasts of the earth. So, if summer is not summer, what is it? And, the same question goes for the harvest; to what is Isaiah referring? We have alluded to these, but let's look at them in detail.

The summers in Israel are very hot. Consequently, a summer became imagery for discipline or persecution by the hand of God. As a person could not escape the summer heat, one could not escape God's persecution or discipline. I believe Isaiah is telling us that terrorists will terrorize until the persecution of judgment by God ends. I believe the time is set based on the length of time we failed to heed His warnings while we pushed for land for peace. That was exactly twenty one years from October 1991 to October 2012. Remember in Chapter Three, we saw Judah and later all of Israel go into captivity and then, the Diaspora for each year the Shmitah years where ignored. We ignored God for twenty one. I think terrorists will *feed* for twenty one months. Concerning the time length of invading nations, we have a measuring stick of sorts.

The beasts of the earth will be here through the harvest. The harvest is definitely not a literal harvest, as we have already eluded. Nor, is it the harvest (rapture and resurrection) of the saved. There is another kind of harvest, a harvest of souls at the end of the age. The imagery is in Joel 3:13 and Revelation 14. The imagery in Revelation is that of grapes of the earth (as opposed to the vine) are worshippers of the Beast (read Islam) are gathered by angels and thrown into the winepress of God. Here, then, is a possible scenario.

As the twenty one months of murder, mayhem and forced conversion to Islam finishes many Americans are now confessed Muslims. Whether they are true believers or did so just to save their lives doesn't matter. Then, by the unseen direction of angels, very unfriendly nations invade America, most likely in different regions. These nations are not Muslim nations. As events play out in the Middle East fulfilling the end times' prophecies, here in America the end times harvest of all Muslims is taking place at unaware agents of God, the invading forces. I believe they will be targeted. Other nations of the world will see the Islamic caliphate as a threat by then. The duration of how long this harvest lasts will be as it was for the birds of prey only this period will be based on how long we continued to squeeze Israel after October 30, 2012. It ends when the final bowls of wrath are poured out and the restoration of all things (Peter speaking in Acts 3:21) are completed. Of course, when they are over it is because Jesus returns and sets up His world-wide rule from Jerusalem. Again, there is no proof for this time frame, only an educated guess. But, I do not have the sense I am very far off.

Verse 7

> *At that time a gift of homage will be brought to the* L*ORD* *of hosts from a people tall and smooth, even from a people feared far and wide, a powerful and*

oppressive nation, whose land the rivers divide–to the place of the name of the LORD of hosts, even Mount Zion. [42]

When it ends there will be survivors, but none with wicked hearts. How many is uncertain, but enough to have the need to form some sort of government and send a delegation to travel back to Israel as representatives of the former unnamed nation. Whether the status of nationhood will still be granted is unknown. Whether the land is called America is anyone's guess. This time, however, we will not be taking some type of leverage to goad Israel to give up God's land. This trip will be the first of many annual trips to pay a gift of homage to King Jesus, who reigns from exactly the location King David reigned four thousand years before; Mount Zion, Jerusalem, Israel. What form the homage takes and how it is to be paid, we are not told.

We can assume this: since Jesus is on David's throne, as promised by God Himself, then we can safely assume He has not only returned, but the Day of Judgment is past. The millennium kingdom has begun. We do not know if complete order has been restored to the world. The world has to be in a bad state following the devastation on the peoples and the land from the judgment of God and the bowls of wrath poured out. We do know it is over. Jesus has taken the Throne as King of Kings and Lord of Lords following His coronation during some future Feast of Tabernacles.

Looking back over the seven verses of Isaiah Eighteen, I had no idea when I started to understand this revelation, how much would be uncovered. I must make the point again that the identity of Isaiah's unnamed nation will not be found to be the United States or America in any commentary or note in your bible. If you were writing a commentary and came to a very short chapter mentioning Cush (Ethiopia) in a vague context, wouldn't you write a few obligatory remarks and move on rather than do the one thing you could not do and that is to leave no comments at all about the chapter and move on. The call and pressure for giving covenant land in exchange for peace is the centerpiece in order for Isaiah's words to make sense; these are very recent events against the scope of time, long after most Commentaries and Study Bibles went to press.

These seven verses and what they portend are not at all uplifting. No one who has fondness for America can be edified by reading this. No one who lives here, citizen or not, after digesting the gravity of these words can have a feeling of security. For those Americans who have deep feeling for our founding, form of government, the role we played in the world through World War II have a difficult time viewing America as an oppressive nation. Unfortunately, in many ways we have been ugly Americans. The statement, "To whom much has been given; much is expected," comes to mind. Who we have been in the past doesn't really count for today. For today, we are judged by God and found to be a nation wanting. We are guilty as one. Is there any hope for individuals when judgment is executed?

The one glimmer of hope is to reach the barn and not be bundled with the tares. To be wheat, one must be producing fruit. Now is the time to be honest with oneself. The comfort zone of living our lives is much more closely to that of tares than we would want to admit to others. The preponderance of words in the New Testament is given as instruction to Christian children. A Christian child can have gone to church all of his life. He may even be in the ministry. They are those not much beyond the early steps of Christian maturity, much less in the early fruit producing stage. How you can begin to produce the fruit of the Spirit is next and it, in itself, is part of a secret. If you are not absolutely sure in your heart you have a close, personal relationship with Jesus, please, read the next chapter with an open mind and a prayer for understanding. Time is too short to be deceived by misguided self—righteousness about being a good Christian.

CHAPTER FIVE: THE NARROW WAY

This is the map of the narrow way

The place of the secret, mentioned when we closed the previous chapter, will be revealed in the next chapter. First, we need to help you identify where you are on the path toward Christian maturity — the fruit producing stage. I think I have found the key to doing just that. One day the Holy Spirit revealed something to me in the Book of 1 John. Like all revelations, I have had from scripture; it came with a 'wow'. It wasn't that it was so monumental; it was that I had not heard it from anyone and it seemed so helpful to anyone walking the narrow path, as opposed to the broad way. What He showed me was that John lays out the tree stages of Christian maturity and provides path markers, like mile markers on an interstate highway, so that anyone can tell where they are along the journey. It is one of those invaluable, hidden nuggets.

The reason it is so valuable is because when growing in the walk to spiritual maturity, it is very helpful to know where you are without subjective assumption. Paul writes in Ephesians ...*until we all attain to the unity of the faith, and of the knowledge of the Son of God, to a mature man, to the measure of the stature which belongs to the fullness of Christ.* [43] That should be the individual goal of each one of us: the fullness of Christ. An immature Christian would shudder at the thought of being seen as trying to attain the fullness of Christ. It would seem almost blasphemous. The reason, I suspect is that they confuse the meaning of the name *Jesus* with the word *Christ*. We are not encouraged to attain the fullness of Jesus, but that of Christ. But what does *Christ* really mean? In fact, what does it mean to be in Christ, or what Paul means by ...*to whom God willed to make known what is the riches of the glory of this mystery among the Gentiles, which is Christ in you, the hope of glory?* [44] We need to take a Rabbit Trail.

Rabbit Trail #1

The word *Christ* is of course Greek. It is the Greek form of the Hebrew word *Messiah*. *Messiah* means Anointed One. What does *anointed* mean? The Hebrews anointed three offices: king, priest and prophet. Prophets anointed other prophets and kings. Priests anointed priests. They did this by smearing a little sanctified oil on the forehead of the one being anointed. Smearing is, in fact the meaning of the word *anointed*. They did this for the same reason we lay hands on people today.

The laying on of hands is done to proclaim and ritualistically pass the power of God on a person. Now the power is not all encompassing — it is the power required to perform the duties of the office. So, if Jesus was the Anointed One, above all others anointed, what was His office and what were His duties? He actually had all three offices. He is the only person to be King, High Priest and Prophet of God. And who anointed Him? The Holy Spirit did at His baptism. (By the way, He was baptized as part of His appointment to the office of High Priest. The main reason Luke goes to so much trouble to establish John the Baptist as being in the priestly line is to show John is qualified to preside at Jesus' appointment. Prior to being robed for his investiture, the High Priest-to-be was required to have a ceremonial washing supervised by a priest. That was why Jesus was baptized.) What were Jesus' duties as Messiah?

His job description is found in Isaiah 61. Remember, Jesus went back to Nazareth and attended the synagogue service described in Luke Chapter Four. He read from Isaiah 61 and said that (what He read) was fulfilled in their hearing. He read the part that specifically addressed what He was to accomplish with the power which the Holy Spirit had clothed Him. This is what He read, "THE SPIRIT OF

THE LORD IS UPON ME, BECAUSE HE ANOINTED ME TO PREACH THE GOSPEL TO THE POOR. HE HAS SENT ME TO PROCLAIM RELEASE TO THE CAPTIVES, AND RECOVERY OF SIGHT TO THE BLIND, TO SET FREE THOSE WHO ARE OPPRESSED, TO PROCLAIM THE FAVORABLE YEAR OF THE LORD." [45] He stopped in the middle of Verse Two of Isaiah. He did not finish reading, "*...AND THE DAY OF VENGEANCE OF OUR GOD;*" He stopped because His commission during his time in his human body did not include these duties. He will accomplish this at His Second Coming. Now, we can get back on track.

The meaning, then, of our purpose in the Christian walk is to be able do what Jesus did in that segment of Isaiah. That is much easier to write than to do. That is why the unity of the faith and the full knowledge of the Son of God is the prerequisite to being a mature man in Christ. Now let me clarify what neither Paul nor I am saying. We are not saying that a Christian can be perfect as Jesus was. If you got that, then go back and read more carefully what was written. It may well defy the traditions in which you are steeped from early teachings. Most all of us have those ropes of traditional thinking tied on some of our thinking. I surely did. One had to do with women.

Rabbit Trail #2

I could not understand why the Bible was so male centric. Yes, I know, it was the culture of the day. Women were to bear the children

Chapter Five: The Narrow Way

and keep the home; two full time jobs at the same time! But why did women seem to be so excluded from God's inclusiveness? I found the answer and, it turns out, He was inclusive after all.

The First Century culture was all about inheritance; wealth, in the form of animals and property, being passed from the father to the sons. The elder son received a double portion; the rest, single. A daughter, when she married, left her father's house (all that he had) and joined her father—in—law's house. If she became widowed, her husband's brother(s) then had the obligation for her support and to marry her for child bearing (the First Century pension plan). If she did not marry and there were no sons, she inherited. Were there brothers, she received an allotment. The focus remained male inheritance.

Jump now to the New Testament. We are not male and female in God's eyes, rather all are sons. In the New Testament, being a son has nothing to do with the sex of a person, it has everything to do with one's inheritance. As God's sons, we are all entitled to our portion of His inheritance, which happens to be all riches in the heavenly realm. The really neat thing about it is that we get it without our Father having to die. While we are on inheritance, let's shift slightly to self—image.

Our Rabbit Trail has lead us directly back to where we need to be to learn from John in his first epistle. I am going to make a bold statement: wherever you are along the path toward spiritual maturity, you have the wrong self—image. How can I possibly know that? It is simple; if you have a self—image; it is not God's image of you. I know, it is a feeble play on words, but it has a cognitive purpose. If we don't see ourselves as God sees us, we are severely short-changing ourselves. Believe me, His is better. Someone found a simple, effective way to change one's self-image to God's image. He simply went through his New Testament and everywhere there was a reference to *you*, he drew a line through it and wrote in his name. Then, every time he read in that section of His Bible, he would read who he was. That makes an indelible impression on the subconscious mind. In time, it becomes the way one thinks of himself. Thus, it enables one to agree with God as to whom you are. Try it, it does wonders for self-esteem. Not to mention the confident authority with which you will rule over the rulers, against the powers, against the world forces of this darkness, against the spiritual *forces* of wickedness in the heavenly *places*.[46] One cannot see oneself as God does without conscious effort. You are going to become the image in your sub-conscious mind.

Chapter Five: The Narrow Way

The characteristics given us by the Apostle John of fathers, young men and little children range from the briefest to the detailed, respectively. He only uses one word to classify those as fathers. It is the word *know*. The definition for this Greek word *ginóskō* means to begin to know, or to know completely, according to the *Enhanced Strong's Lexicon*. In *Louw—Nida* 28.1, [47] it says, "This verb is variously nuanced in contexts relating to familiarity acquired through experience or association with person or thing." So, a father, as defined by John, knows and understands God very well, not only through study and observation about Him, but on an intimate basis through association. A person one knows in this way, one held up as a role model, is one who is respected. Out of honor to that person, one does what the role model asks. [1 John 2:3] John only has three characteristics for young men.

Young men, the apostle says, are strong, and the word of God abides in them, and they have overcome the evil one. [48] The word *strong* here does not mean physical strength. It means these Christians, male and female, have learned the endurance of steadfastness. Through the application of faith in their lives, the have learned to remain focused on the image of the hope of the promise of the word until it materializes in this natural realm: until it becomes reality. That is spiritual strength. In doing so, the word of God not only is something they have read, studied and meditated on, but it has reached the point that it has a life of its own within them. It is beginning to dictate the way they live their lives, no longer a life of response to the demands of the old nature. They no longer have to think about what the word says to do; it is what they do, naturally. Through these two sea changes of living, they have overcome the evil one. The grasp of this world; the lust of the flesh, the lust of the eyes and the boastful pride of life [49] no longer has a hold on them. Their mind has been renewed, as Paul describes in Romans 12:2, 2 Corinthians 4:16, Ephesians 4:23 and Colossians 3:10. [1 John 3:13b, 14b]

Rabbit Trail #3

If you have not closely read the story of the Exodus, there are many things of which you may not be aware. The biggest is that the exodus is a foreshadowing of the Christian walk. But, that is not what I want to point out here.

Exodus gives us an edifying lesson in sin. Here is how. The word *Egypt* also means two borders. Egypt did, in fact, effectively have two borders. The area along the Nile basin was where the main population resided and where the majority of the army was housed. This was the inner border. Across the arid land to the east, traveling to about the location of today's Suez Canal, one would come to their

Chapter Five: The Narrow Way

outer border. In between there were few towns. Succoth was one, where Joseph's bones were buried. Mostly, there were just military outposts in proximity to watch towers. One of these would have been at Migdol, where they crossed the Red Sea (today's Gulf of Aqaba). Here is the parallel.

When anyone first comes to the Lord, they, by Grace, are translated out of the Kingdom of Darkness and placed in the Kingdom of Light. The Kingdom of Darkness is a place of bondage, corruption and death. It is a real spiritual place. The plight of the children of Jacob, to whom Moses returned to deliver, were slaves to Pharaoh; just as everyone born with a human father's DNA is a slave to sin. That is, until a person believes in the name of Jesus. If you remember, Jesus, in Hebrew, is *Yeshua*. The word means salvation. Until a person believes in salvation through the personal work of Jesus in His life, death and resurrection (the Bible says believe on His name; means the same thing) and confess Him as their Lord (thus, replacing Satan as their de facto lord), they cannot be saved. When they do, they leave slavery, just as the children did. That does not mean that sin no longer continues its influence over them. A young Christian is between the inner and outer border. And that is where John's little children are found; delivered from the ultimate penalty of sin but still under its influences and consequences.

Most of John's letter, as you might imagine is addressed to this group. Found in 1 John is the guideposts by which one can tell if they are a member of this group. The first of these have to do with where one walks. By walk, and Christian walk, the scriptures mean lifestyle.

A danger sign is when one wanders between the two lifestyles. Trying to do what you think is God's way works for a while and then the flesh raises its demands and one is back in the familiar land of darkness. [1 John 1:6] These two will compete for a while, but eventually, the heart will become hardened and darkness will begin to win out. Remember, those of the Exodus wanted to return to slavery, but Moses held them in check. How can one break out of this secondary bondage? The only way is to renew the mind with God's word. The Christian lifestyle is not one people can self-will to live. It is like a spring, or fountain, bubbling forth a God-like lifestyle from within.

Jesus said, "...the words that I have spoken to you are spirit and they are life." [50] Prior to the confession of belief, in the truth of who Jesus is, a person's spirit has no life generating force. It is incapable of reaching God's life, no matter how good a life the person thinks he is leading. When this person's bodily function, that we know as life, ceases their spirit can only go to one place; that of darkness, because it does not have the generating power of eternal life where there is Light (God). Once the eternal life comes into their heart (spirit), it comes as a spiritual seed. Natural seeds need water, minerals and sunlight to germinate and continue to grow. God's word supplies all three, in a spiritual sense and the seed of salvation (eternal life) is sustained. Over time, it will germinate and grow. Eventually, it will become a spiritual plant able to produce God Fruit (fruit of the Spirit); something of which the natural man is totally incapable. This is one of the test questions as to where one is along the spiritual pathway. Is sin still an <u>active</u> influence in your life, not an occasional oops?

Another common trap to young Christians is self—righteousness. By the way, remember none of this has anything to do with how long a person has been a Christian. All of it this is outside any timeline that measures age. There are a couple of warning signs of self—righteousness. The biggest is judgment of another. It goes something like this internally: What that person is doing is ungodly. If you stop here it is not judgment; rather, discernment, a holy quality. If the thought continues to they should be punished, now it is becoming judgment. The thoughts go on; however, that they should have (names some negative things happening in the life of the person as a punishment for their actions), because that is what they deserve. The formula is: judged, found guilty and sentenced. [1 John 1:8]

Self-righteousness stems from pride. Self-righteous people are judgmental, critical of other's behavior, fault finders. Inwardly, they don't see their own sin is the same as what they condemn. Thus, without the word of Truth to correct them, they avoid repentance and are self—deceived, according to John. Both the lack of reading, studying and meditating on the word and a self—righteous nature lead to the third telltale sign John gives us for little children.

A little child in Christ is in a constant struggle to keep God's commandments. This is not quite the same thing as being pulled back into the darkness, being under the influence of sin. This has to do with wanting to keep them for the wrong motive. The wrong motive is to keep them because Christians are supposed to keep them and it is important to look pious to one's friends. The right motive is to keep them because they are God's and out of respect for and honor to Him, they are just done, usually without conscious thought. The worst thing about a person sinning, and ultimately failing to keep His commandments is just this, it pains God to witness it. To begin to grasp, just to begin to grasp, how awful sin is to God, look what Jesus endured in humiliation, suffering, pain and agony when He confronted the curse of sin on the cross. The proper motivation to

Chapter Five: The Narrow Way

not sin is not because Christians are not supposed to, it is because a Christian sinning dishonors, disrespects and separates himself from our Father. It hurts Him. When one begins to have that as motivation, that person is growing in Christian maturity. [1 John 2:9, 10]

Rabbit Trail #4

The immediate damage to the one who sins is that a spiritual barrier suddenly is erected between the person and God. John says it this way, "Beloved, if our heart does not condemn us, we have confidence before God. And whatever we ask we receive from Him because we keep His commandments and do the things that are pleasing in His sight." [51] Now let me compare this verse with one from the Apostle Mark. This verse follows as Jesus is explaining to the disciples that faith has the power to move a mountain. (This by the way is a Jewish idiom meaning that one has to do a very difficult thing. Jesus is not being literal about casting mountains into the sea. Unfortunately, I am afraid this misunderstanding has caused many Christians to tune out to believing faith. They would like to have it, but who has ever heard of anyone moving a mountain by faith?) He goes on to say, "...Therefore I say to you, all things for which you pray and ask, believe that you have received them, and they will be *granted* you." [52] Looking at these two verses, the instruction is:

1. Prayers from a believer with un-confessed sin are ineffective, but not because of God.
2. Those prayers cannot be believed as being already answered, because of the unseen barrier; the lack of confidence resulting in ineffectiveness.

In its most basic definition, biblical belief is total confidence. [1 John 5:14, 15]

There is one other thing important thing about prayer. This from Philippians, Paul writes, "Be anxious for nothing, but in everything by prayer and supplication with thanksgiving let your requests be made known to God."[2] There are two things here. First, the word *supplication* means an urgent pleading. The second is the expression of the word *thanksgiving*. It is fruitless to ask for something outside God's will. The offer of thanksgiving is the work of faith (faith without works is dead). The faith part is the conviction that because God said it, through a written promise in our *ketubah*, He has already begun the manifestation of the answer to the prayer. (If you do not know the meaning of the word *ketubah*, please read Appendix B. It is about Christian foreshadowing in the Jewish wedding. You will even find information on the rapture.)

This is helpful in improving one's prayer life, but exactly what does the Bible mean when it says to keep God's commandments?

Chapter Five: The Narrow Way

The Old Testament has 613. Are we to keep all of them? The short answer is no. Have you forgotten the Christian lifestyle is not regulated by the will of doing/not doing, but from a Godly nature within? God's commandments to us are simple and two-fold. We are to believe everything the Bible says about who Jesus is. In doing so the vertical relationship between the individual and God is established. Then, we are to love others. [1 John 3:23] The God way to love another is not emotional; it is willful. We will discuss Christian love more a little later and I will give you the Bible's outline of what love is and what love is not.

The Apostle has another helpful warning to the little child Christian against being self-deceived as to thinking they are a dispenser of God's love. It is nothing more than having hate inside for someone else. To hate someone means to dislike strongly, with the implication of aversion and hostility. This definition is from *Louw Nida* 88.198. 1 John draws the connection of hate and murder. Hate and love will not exist in a side—by—side relationship. [1 John 3:15]. God made everyone and therefore, honor is due every man. Moreover, Jesus died for everyone. Understand this, especially those who defend self or others, killing a person and murdering a person is not the same thing. We are talking here of murder. There is no penalty in killing.

The hate has to go. The way to do that is to confess the fact hate is there and give it to Jesus. Some people confess it while writing it on a slip of paper. Then, wad the paper up throw it away, symbolically giving it to Jesus. When the thought of hate is presented again about that person, immediately the action of writing, wadding and throwing will return. When it does, say out loud that hate toward that person has been given to Jesus and it will be no longer entertained as a thought or emotion. For good measure, declare that it is bound from returning.

When the knowledge of forgiveness is not completely settled in the mind of a little child Christian, it is a certain indication they are still between the borders; not yet completely having put the sin lifestyle behind them. This occasional doubt indicates a believer does not yet have a full grasp on the reality of the gospel in their lives. A person who does not feel comfortable evangelizing another person doesn't yet have the gospel as a reality in their spirit. Curry Blake, Overseer of John G. Lake Ministries, says it this way, "Until the Gospel is real to you; you cannot make it real to another." They have head knowledge; they can answer all the test questions, but what happened in the atonement is not yet real to their lives. Until it is, they cannot become John's young man Christian. They must focus on what Jesus did for them in His scourging, in the shedding

Chapter Five: The Narrow Way

of His blood on the cross and His victorious work in Hell until those become part of them. These are the elements of the atonement. If the Spirit is convicting you as you are reading, imagine you were there. In your imagination see, feel, hear and smell the atonement. You will have it when what Jesus suffered is as real as if were happening before your eyes. [1 John 4:9 — 11]

Another blockade for the little child Christian is a continued fixation and fascination with the world. [1 John 2:15—17] As a result, they look at reality and the facts it presents, barely aware of God's Word and the Truth it presents. The facts of the present will change; the Truth of the word remains forever. The symptom of this condition is when facts are accepted as truth. The little child Christian may know and confess the Word over the facts, but nothing changes. Deep down, Truth is no more real to them than the facts. Now, those of you familiar with the word of Faith movement may read this and think I am promoting it. I am not. The Word of Faith is built on confession, usually related to finances or health. Confession without unshakeable belief in a clearly written and witnessed Biblical promise is very dangerous. It will damage the confessor's image of themselves, bring into question about the nature of God from those around him and probably line the pockets of somebody else. It always comes out of the person's will and not produced by the Spirit.

Another area has to do with the anointing. [1 John 2:20, 27] We have discussed what the anointing is; the power of God behind one to perform a specific job. The little child Christian will wait on God to call him into service. No calling from God is necessary as it already is your job description. Just do it, as the sport's company encourages. The anointing follows the act of faith. One must believe it will be there to enforce what one says and does. In fact, the little children do not walk by faith (it is not their lifestyle), but they attempt to exercise faith in their lives. In most cases, it is unrealized if they were honest with themselves. The reason is because they turn out to be false witnesses. Here is what I mean.

1. Palm 119:89 says that forever, O Lord, your word is settled in heaven.
2. 2 Corinthians 13:1 expands on Deuteronomy 19:15 saying that everything must be confirmed by two or more witnesses.
3. When a person stands on God's word, they are in the Court of Truthfulness (already established). Trials, tests and/or temptations are the cross-examiners.
4. If the confession of the promise is maintained, the person is found to be a faithful witness and the ketubah is honored. If

not, the witness found to be a false witness, a harlot under the ketubah and not worthy of the promise it grants.

Jesus, in Matthew 12: 33—37, makes a point so profound that, because of its brevity, it may be easily missed. He starts by giving a natural example: trees are good or bad by the fruit they produce. Then, evil men can't unconsciously speak good words because out of the sub-conscious mind (heart) unguarded words will reveal one's true nature. The unconscious is where a person has hidden what is truly important to him. For that reason, every unguarded word spoken reveals who you are and that is the person who will be held accountable when judged, not the person the world is shown in guarded moments. It is these words alone, not actions (which follow the words), that either justify a person or condemn him. Looking back on 1 — 3, above, do you see why faith does not work? It is because, when tested, the person does not maintain by spoken words what the Bible says. If a person does not say what the Bible says about a subject — in which he previously said he believes — that makes him a liar, because he has not spoken Truth. God faith only produces God hope.

A very important characteristic of little children is they are givers, not takers. [1 John 3:17] This fundamental characteristic of God's character is a litmus test for anyone who wonders whether they have been saved. Always look to one's character. If it is not like God's, if His character (nature) is not the predominant characteristics in one's own nature, then the red flags should go up. All of the other things may not be learned, but the core — the nature of character- is present.

Having this nature does not insure the little child yet understands the spiritual place they now occupy. They do not yet understand their authority, the role in the Kingdom they are to play. In such an early state, and then, even later in the advancing walk, there is a telltale indicator. That indicator is fear. [1 John 4:17, 18]

Fear is a sure fire indicator there is work yet to be done. I am not talking about the fight or flight response in self-preservation, rather the fear that lingers. When the Evil One has been overcome, John's definition of the Young Man, fear is displaced by the certain knowledge God loves you. If God loves you, there is a promise that all things will work together for good for those who love Him AND are called according to His purpose. His purpose is that the believer be conformed to the same image of His Son. [52] There is a line in a wonderful, secular movie entitled *The Most Exotic Marigold Hotel*. [53] It is this, "Everything will be good in the end. And, if it is not good, it is not yet the end." For me, that sums up my internal response when fear tries to raise its ugly head and come against my faith. For me it is a powerful antidote against fear. I know that no matter what happens to me, in the end, I have eternity in the presence of God.

We have come to John's last alert for one who is a little child. It is this: guard yourself from idols. [54] It is the last line He wrote. The word *idol* in the Bible means any image, real or imagined, setup by an individual to be worshipped. The word *worship*, in its most simple definition means to express by attitude and possibly by position one's allegiance to and regard for deity. [55] The warning here is to not put anything ahead of God. The devotion of attention to a thing or thought elevated in position or esteem above God is an idol. Why is this so dangerous? Of all the things which John gave as instructions to move from being a little child to a young man, this is the only warning against demonic influence. Ask the Holy Spirit to issue a warning should this become an issue for you. Every time afterward, when this warning is presented as a thought, remember to check with God to see if the danger zone has been encroached. If so, carry out some spiritual warfare against the intruder or potential intruder. Get the idol out of your life! [1 John 5:21]

This brings to a close the instructions from John on how to tell if you are, or not, a little child. I have tried to provide practical suggestions on how to master each of these so that you can quickly move on to the next phase, that of young man. Almost certainly, God has already been working in your life to help you with these. He does this because He loves you, though at the time, it may not have seemed like it. How He did this was to have caused something that happened in your life and you did not realize it was from Him. What I am talking about is the discipline a believer receives from God.

Rabbit Trail #5

The Book of Hebrews has a most interesting revelation concerning God's discipline of believers. It reads, in part, "MY SON, DO NOT REGARD LIGHTLY THE DISCIPLINE OF THE LORD, NOR FAINT WHEN YOU ARE REPROVED BY HIM; FOR THOSE WHOM THE LORD LOVES HE DISCIPLINES, AND HE SCOURGES EVERY SON WHOM HE RECEIVES." [56] The reason this is in small caps is because it is actually a combination quotations from other verses. They appear originally in other places in the Bible. They are pulled together here. In doing so, they more easily allow the Holy Spirit to show us the revelation. When you see this in your bible, pay special attention to it. If a quote is in all capital letters, as opposed to the small capital letters above, it is an Old Testament scripture quoted in the New Testament. Let's now talk about the word *discipline* in the scripture above.

Discipline appears twice. Once it means reprove and once scourging. In the Greek, two different words for discipline are used. There is a progressive severity in God's discipline. When God disciplines the believer, God first instructs through His word (the Bible). Secondly, He reproves with the word of another. Sometimes, this is from a believer and sometimes not. Sometimes spoken; sometimes written. If the message is not received, then He will make life really uncomfortable. Situations in one's life will really go south, usually in an area that can be related back to the area He is trying to address. If that doesn't work, the cycle will be repeated. (If you haven't noticed, God is cyclical in His creation. Nothing totally ends; it just cycles to begin anew.) Some people think this discipline is only because of sin. I believe not so. Experience has shown me it is to move one along the path of spiritual maturity in whatever area needs to be corrected. There is a statement of which I am fond: God is more concerned with one's character than one's comfort. I don't know who to credit for first saying it.

One final thought before we move on to finding the secret place. This has to do with naysayers. These are self—appointed people whose task is to find fault with another person's ministry. I am not speaking here about being wrong about the fundamentals of the faith or a false prophet. I am speaking about someone who criticizes over doctrinal issues or just has an active critical spirit. If you are the kind of person who likes verification of what someone says by the affirmation of almost all others, you will be limited in the amount of rich spiritual food you are able to receive. Anyone who speaks boldly on a controversial spiritual subject is a magnet for these people.

Having said that, I am not saying to blindly accept everything you read, whether you agree with it or not. It you only expose yourself to what agrees with your understanding, your mind is closed. Learning is impossible with a closed mind. On the other hand, because it is said or written by a supposed authority doesn't make it right either. So how is one to know? The answer is spiritual discernment. However, if you didn't know that from the start of this last thought, your spiritual discernment is most likely not well developed. Ask and believe the Holy Spirit to develop the gift within you. As it develops, fall back on the companionable, friendly umpire; God's Peace, who is found in Philippians 4:7: And the peace of God, which surpasses all comprehension, will guard your hearts and your minds in Christ Jesus. [57] Ask God to give you comfort if what you see, hear or read is true and to disturb you if it is false. He works for you every time you have faith He will.

We have covered quite a bit of ground spiritually. Most likely there are some areas to improve. I urge you to get after those areas. Get into the Bible. If you don't like your translation, find one that you do. Write notes in your bible; the words are sacred, not the paper on which they are printed. But, by all means, supplement any

Bible with at least one concordance. Study bibles and commentaries are wonderful, as long as you realize almost all have a doctrinal slant. If you are sensitive to doctrine, you can disregard that portion. Unfortunately, most of us are not.

May I share with you what I think is the best resource for bible study? It is what I use. Unfortunately, today it is not inexpensive. I bought it years ago and the upgrades have not been too expensive for me to keep abreast, but it is a wonderfully efficient tool. It is Logos Bible Software. Information is available at www.logos.com. There are online Bibles which allow limited word searches. The important point to take away is to add tools to your study. The most important is one that helps you with the meaning of words. You already have the greatest teacher known to man, the Holy Spirit, but remember He is a gentleman and will not teach unless invited. Now, let's see what He wants to teach us about the secret place. You see, He is actually the author of this book, drawing out from me what He has taught me before. I am simply a scribe.

Thanks to the Apostle John, you should have a good notion as to where you are along the path toward spiritual maturity. It is not shameful to be a little child, no matter how long one has been a Christian. If you were ignorant that you were, that was your innocent state. However, now you know. The responsibility to advance farther along the path becomes your own. The free pass for ignorance goes out the window when the breeze of knowledge enters.

When students enter a university, they are (or, in my case, used to be) confronted with a catalogue listing the courses offered by each department or college. These courses have numbers, which designate their level of study. They begin with Number 101 and then advance numerically. For our purposes, think of what has just been presented as a 101 class. Now let's take the next class which will prepare us for advanced, practical studies. We will call it Path to Christian Maturity 102. With 101 successfully behind you, we are ready to matriculate.

CHAPTER SIX: THE GARDEN OF THE SECRET PLACE

Jesus dwelled in the secret place of the Most High

There is a psalm, perhaps you know it. Perhaps, it is one of your favorites and often quoted verses. It is Psalm 91. It starts off: He who dwells in the secret place of the Most High shall abide under the shadow of the Almighty. [58] As the psalmist continues, he proclaims that his refuge and fortress of protection is God. And, he trusts God to provide for his security. The verses following are a litany of disasters, all of which are prevented by God from coming to pass in the psalmist's life. It ends with God proclaiming His devout protection and promise of salvation.

Now watch closely, all protection in this psalm depends on the first ten words. No guaranteed protection from God is available to anyone who does not dwell in His secret place. In the story of the wheat and tares, [59] only the wheat is carried into the barn. The tares were bundled for burning. The wheat, growing among the tares, was actually dwelling in the secret place of the Most High. He who abides there dwells under the active protection of the Living God. The evidence was their production of grain. I have wondered if the tares ever noticed they were without grain (fruit). Jesus mentions in Matthew 7: 21-23 that many seemed shocked, crying out Lord, Lord when denied entrance into Heaven. Their plea for entry was based on the works they had done. Jesus rejected them because He did not know them. The reason: they had not done His Father's will.

Going to church your whole life is not dwelling in the secret place. Being born into a Christian family is not dwelling in the secret place. Being confirmed after Confirmation Class is not dwelling in the secret place. Joining the church is not dwelling. Asking Jesus to come into your heart at the altar of your church is not. Nor, does dwelling mean being a good person, helping others, supporting causes with money or service. There is one way and one way only to dwell in the secret place of the Most High. The psalmist told us how in seven words. He said, "My God, in whom I will trust." It sounds simple and easy; it's not. So let's find out why it is not and practical steps to find the secret place. Until it is found, obviously, one can't dwell there.

In order to find the secret place of the Most High, one must look for it; and look in the place where it can be found. Arkansas

Chapter Six: The Garden of the Secret Place

Diamond State Park is the only diamond field in the United States. If you want to find a diamond in nature and don't look there, you are wasting your time. Likewise, with the secret place; the secret place is found in the Kingdom of God. I am, of course, not talking about a part on the earth. Rather, the meaning of our prayer, thy Kingdom come, thy will be done on earth as it is in Heaven. [60] It is already here and in its garden is the secret place. To access the Kingdom, special credentials are required. Think of them as gardening clothes.

We have been taught for one to reach salvation, just follow Romans 10: 9, 10; confess and believe. There is a caveat in the word believe. Today, in America, *believe* has the preponderance of meaning to be that of mental accent. Something like, yes, that sounds correct. I believe that. No action is required to verify the belief. The biblical meaning is two part; confession with corresponding action. The colloquial phase is; don't just talk the talk, but also walk the walk. Saying Jesus is the Lord of your life (verse nine in Romans Ten) does not make Him so. Going on to do what He says makes Him Lord. When Jesus is confessed as Lord, the person making it places himself voluntarily in a position of servant ship under Him. The person becomes the willing slave to do whatever the Master says. The Bible calls this a bond servant, i.e., servant by choice. Free will is no longer an option. Jesus teaches a practical lesson in how this obedience is acquired in Luke 6: 45, 46.

He has been teaching lessons He taught when delivering the Sermon on the Mount back in Matthew's gospel beginning in the fifth chapter. Now He is teaching lessons from nature proving the Law of Reproduction: a like thing produces a like thing. Apples produce apples, grapes produce grapes, etc. Then He says this, "The good man out of the good treasure of his heart brings forth what is good; and the evil *man* out of the evil *treasure* brings forth what is evil; for his mouth speaks from that which fills his heart. Why do you call Me, 'Lord, Lord,' and do not do what I say?"[3] This is the way I understand it; no one can do what He says as one's way of life if what He says is not rooted in their heart beforehand.

Let's now see how it works out in the real world. Go to Mark Four and the story of the sower sowing the seed. Here are the players:

- The sower — anyone speaking the word of God from a heart of belief (Jesus' representative)
- The seed — the word of God
- The ground — a person's heart; the place inside where the you resides, your spirit, the seat of character and motive
- Packed down soil by the road — a spirit unwilling to listen to the word

Chapter Six: The Garden of the Secret Place

- Rocky ground — a spirit of little substance who likes the sound of the word but abandons it when pressures of life heats up and contradicts the word
- Ground with thorns — the most threatening to the seed's life
  - Worries of the world (things one sees or hears in the natural which, to him, are more believable than the promises of God)
  - Deceitfulness of riches (joy of living is in financial security and dependence on the provider, like an employer or one's talent)
  - Desires for other things (hearing, studying, meditating the word is not as desirable to do as most anything else)

Remember, we are talking about doing what Jesus says. If what He says is not the dominant thing in one's consciousness, if attention focuses on other things when the opportunity to focus on Him presents itself throughout the day, if there is no conversation with Him, only occasionally thinking about Him, no asking Him questions and listening for answers, no meditating on what the lesson is for you from the Bible beyond just what the text says, then fruit is not going to produce. There was nothing planted from which to produce.

In all likelihood what life will be is religious (not a good thing). A religious person focuses on self-doing, not on the relationship with God. The *many* in Matthew Seven were religious. There will be submerged sin: judgment of others, jealousy, unforgiveness, anger, greed, eager to gossip and a whole lot of self-righteousness. In a word, a heart full of evil. Way back in our discussion of Isaiah 18, we said the remnant have no wickedness in their heart. For these people, talking about Jesus in religious settings pleases; talking to Jesus one on one never is on the day's schedule. The criteria for doing for others are weighed against getting benefits to self. The quid pro quo is always a consideration. If one's life view is to live the world's way, the world's way is the life which is lived.

Thus, this business of being a Christian has nothing to do with the label. It has everything to do with the motivation of the life. The will of God is for us to love one another (1 Thessalonians 4: 9, among others). This kind of love is, of course, God's kind of love. It is not emotional, i.e., prompted by a feeling. It is an act of the will, coming out of self—discipline. The definition of this kind of love has seven things to do and eight things to not do. Here they are from 1 Corinthians 13: 4-8:

Love is:

- ❖ Patient
- ❖ Kind
- ❖ Rejoices with truth

Chapter Six: The Garden of the Secret Place

- ❖ Bears all things (doesn't say things about a person that would be hurtful to them)
- ❖ Believes all things (sees others the way God sees them)
- ❖ Hopes all things (another's spiritual man mirroring God's image of him will emerge)
- ❖ Endures all things (is not dissuaded from good conquering evil)
- ❖ Never found to fail

Love is not:
- ❖ Jealous
- ❖ Braggadocios
- ❖ Arrogant
- ❖ Rude
- ❖ Seeking only one's own kind
- ❖ Easily provoked to anger
- ❖ Keeping a record of a wrong suffered at the hand of another
- ❖ Rejoice with unrighteousness (takes pleasure at another's undeserved misfortune)

Since this is our command for the way to relate to all other people, it might do well to memorize them. We might put them on a card and contemplate them daily, visualizing ourselves relating to others in these ways until they become who we are. Study them until they produce the action in reflex, without thought. Then, and only then, we will be obeying the command. Understand these actions, though they come out of the will, do have a spiritual force to drive them. It is compassion. Compassion does not act based on desire; rather, it acts based on the need to receive on the part of recipient. We now have the formula to do God's will. Now, what about trusting God?

Saying we trust God doesn't mean we really trust God. Sure, He can do anything. Trust, however, always answers in the affirmative the question; will He do it for me right now? Trust is taking action when the Holy Spirit's quiet voice tells you to do so and the circumstances about you are telling you no, no, no. Trust has a twin named faith. Trust is acting on belief; faith is acting on a promise. You may know faith as part of the armor. It is the shield. Trust is something which grows out of you. Faith is something given to you, but you must use it. Let's explore faith, because it is the one thing, that when we exercise it, pleases God.

Faith is one of those words having a different meaning in the context used. When we say something like, "I am of the faith," doctrinal issues are generally meant. When we say, "My faith is in Christ," we are really saying that we have trust for salvation. When we say, "I have faith for (any of God's promises to us)," that is

Chapter Six: The Garden of the Secret Place

the meaning with which I want us to concentrate and to become comfortable.

You have heard it said, and truthfully so, that the Bible defines itself. And, so it is with faith. The definition is found in Hebrews 11: 1, 2. It reads, "Now, faith is the substance of things hoped for; the conviction of things not seen." The word *now* is an interesting word to start the sentence. I mentioned before the time of Heaven is now. One of the characteristics of our realm is time. One of the characteristics of eternity is the absence of time. If Heaven had a time, it would be now, eternally. Faith is of that realm, the kind of faith we are talking about. It is the spiritual foundation of this entire created universe. It, therefore, is something everyone has while alive. Atheists have faith. Perhaps their faith is in mankind, science or themselves. They have the expectation of hope in something. Faith always works, always, unless contaminated by doubt.

Faith, then, is not a religious word. Being the means of creation, the laws that govern faith always apply. The first law is that a concept must be envisioned. Envisioned is the operative word. It, the hope, must be something which can be seen or envisioned in the mind's eye. Second, that vision must be put into words and spoken. Third, the certainty that the words which have been spoken will materialize, the way they were envisioned, into reality in this realm.

This is accomplished by reinforcing daily with reading, speaking and hearing every lesson the Bible teaches concerning this hope. Pausing to *see* the hope materialized now. Fourth, the steadfast maintenance of the image envisioned is consistently held, even though it can't yet be perceived in this reality and never contradicted by a spoken word. If a contradicting word does slip and something is uttered to the contrary, immediately rebuke those spoken words and render them inoperable. What is spoken as a promise of faith must align itself with God's will. That is how creation came into being. An attentive reading of Genesis One reveals this. God had a vision of what He wanted. He had a word for it and spoke the word. He believed what He said would materialize and it did. Money or an item of barter have a perceived value and are commodities of exchange in this world. Faith is the commodity of exchange in the spiritual realm. Only the Law of Depletion is inverted. In the natural, the more money one spends, the less he has. The more one *spends* their faith, the richer they become. Jesus, the Bible tells us, lived by faith — His way of life.

We can see this in many places. First, in just one of several scriptures, Hebrews 11: 6 makes this point about faith when it says that without faith it is impossible to please Him. And then, in Matthew 3:7, during Jesus' baptism, when He came up out of the water, God

Chapter Six: The Garden of the Secret Place

---

speaks from Heaven saying, "This is my son, in whom I am well pleased." If Jesus wasn't living by faith, God could not have been well pleased with him. Realize this is at the start of the ministry. No miracles had been performed, as yet. But shortly afterward, we see it demonstrated at the wedding in Cana, as told by John at the beginning of the Second Chapter of his gospel account. This story is so good, I just have to, at least, sketch it out for you.

The baptism is over and Jesus and His disciples return from the Jordan River and come back to Galilee to a village near Nazareth to attend his younger half-sister's wedding, Mary and Joseph's daughter. We can surmise it is her wedding because John says that Jesus is a guest, but Mary is there. She was not invited, thus a member of the bridegroom or bride's wedding party. As the wedding is in Cana, not Nazareth, she is most likely to be the bride's mother. A calamity happens.

At some point in the festivities, the wine runs out. This is significant because in this First Century culture, to not be able to provide for one's guests was a sign of great disfavor from God. For such a thing like this to happen during your son's wedding was worse. A whole year had been allotted the bridegroom's father to prepare for this event. He, the father, was the one who said when it would happen and now, to run out of wine was unthinkable. The entire family would have been shamed in Cana for the rest of their lives. Mary's daughter would be a part of that family. This is where the idea of giving away the bride comes; the bride's father gives her away to the bridegroom and she becomes a part of his father's family. When a Jewish girl married, she left her father's house (family) and joined her father-in-law's.

In this case, Mary was in on the secret, looming catastrophe from the start. This is another clue this wedding is that of Jesus' sister. We are witnesses to a very human drama playing out. Before the friend of the father, who had been put in charge of all details of the festivities, was told about the depletion of the supply of wine, Mary knew. He is the headwaiter or wine steward in the biblical account. Mary knew, because her daughter, the bride, told her. That is what girls do; they go to their moms in times of stress and distress. Her daughter must have been frantic, but trying to remain calm on the outside. To borrow a legal phrase, time is now of the essence. If the headwaiter finds out, the risk of it being known to the village is very great. If anything can be done to avert disaster for this family, it must be done immediately.

Mary comes straight to Jesus and tells Him the news. I don't believe she had to think about doing this. Conditioned response over the years had taught her that when her life's circumstances were

Chapter Six: The Garden of the Secret Place

without viable options, go to Jesus. His response is strange to us when we read it, but what He basically said was I can't do anything, because I don't have any authority here; it is the bridegroom's father with the authority. But Mary did not come to Him because she thought that Jesus had the authority, she came to Him because she had learned Jesus' way of life produced things that were needed. In other words, He lived by faith. He did not see the problem, rather, the promise. She saw trouble and she came to Him to avert it, she did not care how He did it. That is the point I wanted to make. It is not spoken of as faith in the story, but that is what we have by example. I won't finish the story, but I want to leave you with just this: the story it is not about the miracle of changing the water into wine; it is about the quantity of wine and what that proved.

The definition in Hebrews, which we left a ways back, says that faith is that awareness of certainty that God's promise is going to happen. It is without doubt. It is the title deed to a hope contained in God's word about something you need. The conviction is yours that it is a reality in your life even though it has not yet materialized. That is faith.

Jesus also had half-brothers, in addition to sisters. The eldest of them was James. After the crucifixion, James became head of the church in Jerusalem. There was no other man alive who had witnessed Jesus' life as intimately. James was the oldest of Mary and Joseph's children. James left us with one written document. We know it as the Book of James. It is a primer for living the Christian life. Of the many wonderful lessons James taught about how to live as a Christian, one of the lessons he addresses has to with the negative effect of doubts when applying faith. He paints a good picture analogy of what doubt does to faith. [61] There is a personal story I want to share that was a lesson to me of how devastating doubt or unbelief can do to the good work of applied faith.

Fairly early in our friendship, my good friend Glynda Lomax Linkous called me on a cold, drizzly Sunday afternoon. She had just received a distressful call from a co–worker whose brother was near death in a local hospital. Glynda was on her way to pray for him and asked me to meet her there. Glynda had given me his room number and I arrived in the corridor outside the room. A group of people were gathered around two doctors blocking my entrance. I backed against the wall, out of the way, but near enough to hear one doctor say that it was doubtful that he (I didn't know who the he was) was going to make it through the night. I thought, "I surely hope that's not the guy we are here to pray for." It turned out that is exactly who it was. I had prayed for very few sick at this point and no one this sick. I whispered to God that this was on Him, it was over my head.

Chapter Six: The Garden of the Secret Place

Without knowing why, I sent the family down to the Chapel to wait while we prayed. The prayer turned out to be less of a prayer than spiritual warfare against his condition. I to this day wonder what the patient, and the family member with him, thought was going on behind the curtain separating them from us. The next morning, Glynda got a call of elation from her friend that her brother was going to be alright.

In my enthusiasm, I shared the story with a friend. He had a sick cousin. This time, I made the call to Glynda and off we went. The family joined us in his bedroom for the prayer. We did said pretty much what we had said at the hospital. The next morning, he died. We couldn't figure out what had gone wrong. We rehashed the two experiences several times. Finally, Glynda saw it. The mother, who was in the room, had made a comment of doubt that all of this would work. Never again have I prayed for anything or anyone in a group where I perceived doubt or unbelief. Besides this personal account of the effect of doubt, what I want to point out here is the warning doubt provides the Believer.

If there is any doubt within, and only you know it, it is a red light flashing. Faith is not going to work because the third law causing it to work has been violated. This is the one that says that the certainty of what had been spoken would surely materialize in this realm. If the certainty is not within, the promise is not real to you. You are dealing with it in the realm of the soul; meaning it is on a mental level; not a spiritual one. You can envision it, but not with certainty that it will come to pass your life at this time. So, how do you turn the flashing light from red to green? Go back to where you got the faith in the first place, the word of God applying to the particular promise.

See, this is the mystery most people miss about faith. They think they must generate their faith. No, no. Faith generates itself. It is a seed. It just needs a heart willing to accept the word as being truer than the facts of current reality. Let me convey this in another way, because this is such a stumbling block for most.

Faith comes by hearing. This means the words concerning the promise must make more than a memorable impression in the mind of a person. Those words must convey the concept of what God has said about the promise. The whole concept then, the vision of what it means as applied to your life, must be meditated on, thought about, seen in your mind's eye as already being in your life, mixing this movie playing in your own mental theater with emotions of how it will make you feel, imagine the smells you would sense if it weren't a movie in the imagination, but happening right then in real life. Repeat the process over and over, until within you, the promise is more real than your natural world is without it. That is when the

Chapter Six: The Garden of the Secret Place

promise has germinated and grown from the promise heard to faith in the promise seen. It can be explained as being formed in one's sub-conscious mind as the promise realized. In the end, doubt is not an enemy but a warning, if you know how to heed the warning.

Our search for the secret place of the Most High, which is hidden in the garden of His kingdom have caused us to dig into the plot of godly salvation as witnessed by doing His will as a way of life. And then, in the plot of the garden next to that one, we uncovered the mystery of how to make biblical faith work every time it is needed. The soil is becoming richer as we dig. I think we are near our secret place. Just a little more digging should do it.

My analogy of digging in garden plots may seem a little simple to you. I used it to make the point of what I wrote about concerning Proverbs 27:2. You remember, where it says that it is the glory of God to conceal a matter and it is the gory of kings to reveal a matter. We are living that proverb out right now in our search for the secret place.

Been to the beach? The kind of beach where the sand is so deep it makes walking a little difficult. Keeping that image, now imagine a house built on the sand with no foundation pillars driven into the earth. Okay, you have figured me out. I am alluding to Jesus when He talked about the foolish man and wise man. When the bible talks about the foundation of someone's house it means the beliefs upon which everything near and dear to that life rests. This is the last thing Jesus says in the Sermon on the Mount. This sermon is about the way to live one's life. These are the things we have been talking about. This is the way a life is lived in the secret place. There is nothing in the sermon that is not important, but there are a couple of points Jesus made that I had to learn and I want to pass those on to you, shortly. First, however, I want us to discuss the bedrock upon which the rock foundation stands.

What we are going to look at now is the very bedrock of the Christian belief. It is known as the Atonement. We have talked about it earlier. It is the total crucifixion from of the trial until the resurrection. I am going to leave out many details and subtleties, because this subject is a book in itself. I want to concentrate on why Christianity is true. It is the foundation of Christian faith. To not have this understanding puts a person in one of two places. The first is in a place that deception and false teachings can misguide; negating the Word. The second is a false belief a person may have that they are saved. Both exist today and probably have been over history. Of everything else that I have written; this is most important.

The Sanhedrin was, among other things, the assembly of Jewish leaders acting as the Supreme Court of Jewish law. Their powers

Chapter Six: The Garden of the Secret Place

were total, up to and including the sentence of death and the carrying out of the execution. An example of this is in Acts 6, 7 and 8 in the death of Stephen. This is the way most trials and convictions were carried out. When it came to the execution of Jesus, the Sanhedrin chose a different option.

The influencing majority of this group feared Jesus, because of his influence among the people. He was seen as a direct threat to their individual position and way of life. Their fear was that if Jesus were allowed to live, He would have had all of Israel on His side. With that kind of following, He could easily cause a revolt to overthrow Rome. After all, wasn't that what the Messiah was to do, deliver the people from oppression? They did not believe He was the Messiah. He did not fit the profile, so to speak. (And this is a warning to those in our day regarding the Second Coming.) So, in the scenario of a war with Rome, were the people to revolt members of the Sanhedrin would have lost power, if not their lives and wealth. Their whole society would have been turned upside down. They could not permit that happening, so they had determined that Jesus of Nazareth had to die. The problem was His popularity. The very reason He was a threat was the very reason of His political strength.

During the days leading up to the Passover, the events surrounding Him were getting out of hand very quickly. He did not come to Jerusalem often, so their best chance to get Him was now. It had to happen fast in order to avoid the people threating their authority. For political cover, they could not be seen by the people as being His executioner. They needed two things. They needed two witnesses who would testify He committed blasphemy, a capital offense. They then needed someone who could turn Him over to the guards immediately, before the people found out about the trial and He had a chance to escape. They found two witnesses and a turncoat and bought all off for their acts of treachery. The two witnesses were never named; the finger man was. He was Judas Iscariot, one of Jesus' twelve disciples; the men who were closest to Him. We may speculate regarding Judas' driving motive, we do not have to his end.

Conviction was secured in the dead of night after Judas had informed them he knew where Jesus would be staying overnight. Before first light while the population was asleep, they came with torches to arrest Him. After a trial of mockery at Caiaphas', the High Priest's house, then to Herod and back to Caiaphas, Jesus was taken on to Pilate, having been convicted of blasphemy, a capital offense under Jewish law. In due time, Pontius Pilate pronounces the sentence of death by crucifixion. The first time one reads the accounts of Jesus' arrest and subsequent trials, one is struck by the lack of defense put forward by Jesus. That is, until the realization

Chapter Six: The Garden of the Secret Place

dawns that He chooses this path. This was what the agony in the Garden of Gethsemane was all about. He chose to die this way because it was the kind of death that would allow Him to fulfill His Father's purpose.

Many times I have heard it said that Jesus did not have to die, that He gave up His life for ours. True, He did die for us. What we miss is that He had to die this way, crucifixion, for it to be for us. Jesus had to become the physical receptor of all that sin is. He had to have it all in order to get rid of it. But there was a huge problem — a Catch 22. He had never sinned. Were He to sin, His sacrifice would be in vain; His death justified and deserved. A conundrum had presented itself; thus, crucifixion. It was so, in order to deceive Satan.

Here is how the deception worked. The Book of Deuteronomy is one of the first five books of the Old Testament, which are known as the Torah. All five comprise what we know as the Law. Deuteronomy lays out the instructions of how things are to happen. Almost tucked away, in the 21st chapter, in the 23rd verse, in parenthesis, is this statement: "anyone who hangs on a tree is the curse of God." From Moses, fifteen hundred years before Jesus was sentenced to die, one of the most important phrases ever uttered for and by God through a man were spoken. With that phrase, it now became legal for Jesus to become sin while being guiltless of sin. The Father would issue a curse on Him, not because of who He was, not because of what He had done, but because of where He was. He was hanging on a tree.

If both were not true, there could be no resurrection. Jesus had to die, shed His blood, and He had to be Sin in order to take it to Hell, where He would be found innocent of Sin and thereby be justified to have authority over it. I have read and heard many discuss why Jesus could not come before He did. I have heard the Roman roads being in place for the gospel to spread, for crucifixion to be the form of state employed capital punishment and to the Roman Pax (peace) which allowed relative safety of travel for the gospel to be spread. All of these belong on the list, but I have never heard this tied to the crucifixion; hung on a tree in order to be cursed. And yes, I believe He died hanging on a tree, not a cross.

The Romans used both methods to crucify. The upright poles we see in the icons of our faith were left in the ground. The cross bar was what the condemned carried to the crucifixion site. Remember, they had just been scourged. That flesh ripping beating left a man incapable of running or fighting. Add to that the burden of dragging the cross piece, eliminated any possibility of meaningful resistance once at the site. This was done whether the cross beam was going on the preset upright or into a pre-gouged slot into a tree. During Jesus' crucifixion, the two thieves talked between themselves and

Chapter Six: The Garden of the Secret Place

with Him. Imagine the three of them, having been through what I have just described, and having the strength to speak loud enough to be heard across many feet of separation. In addition, each breath of air came with rotation of one's feet and legs on the spike driven into the ankle and small foot rest for one foot to lift the body up enough to take air into the lungs. They barely had enough air to breath, much less enough extra to force a voice loud enough to carry over many feet. The struggle for air is how people died. When they no longer had the strength to raise their bodies to breathe or their lings filled with water or when their legs were broken to hasten death then they died. These three were not, I believe, separated by many feet with Jesus being in the middle. Remember John's account when the soldier came to break their legs. He went to one and then to the other and then to Jesus, who was already dead. Just mentally picture that happening in our iconic configuration with Jesus in the middle and see if that is the order in which you would have gone had you been that soldier. It just doesn't seem logical to me. And that is not all.

I wondered for years, heard and read many explanations of the water and the blood flowing out of Jesus' side after the soldier reached Jesus. To be certain He was dead, the soldier drove his spear into Jesus' side. Water and blood flowed out. I could never remember those explanations of the meaning of the water and the blood. Finally, it dawned on me to ask God. Within a week, studying for some other purpose, I came across the following:

> Not much imagination is needed to envision the amount of blood generated at Passover from all the lambs who were sacrificed. In order to deal with washing away the blood, the Jews had built large cisterns underneath the Temple floor. They were filled by underground springs. The blood was collected under the alter leading to a large drain which led to the outer wall and dumped into the Hinnon Valley. After the last sacrifice, the High Priest would sacrifice the Passover lamb and declare in a loud voice, *it is finished*, meaning the Passover sacrifices for the year were over. Those are also Jesus' last words. (Remember, as far as the Father is concerned, since His baptism, Jesus is now the lawful High Priest.) Jesus meant there was no more need for any more sacrifices, ever. Then, at the High Priest's declaration, the water in the cisterns was released washing the blood pooled below the sacrificial alter down a drain hewn in the rock and on out through the wall into the valley. Blood and water do not easily mix.

Chapter Six: The Garden of the Secret Place

> When the citizens saw the water and the blood separately flowing out, they knew the sacrifices were completed.

I haven't forgotten this explanation. This valley was also the city garbage dump. It was where the unclaimed bodies were thrown. This applied to the executed who could not immediately be buried. I leave that thought for your contemplation.

The word atonement, of course, means compensation for a wrong. It has the concept of appeasing a deity. Some synonyms are expiation and propitiation, both of which are used in the Bible. When it comes to the work Jesus did on the cross, the three words combined are pitifully weak in definition. No words are sufficient. It is not easy for the human mind to grasp the gravitas of His act. He willfully submitted to humiliation; the Son of God, having to stand wrongfully accused and then judged by flawed men. He bore the degradation of a brutish beating, enduring slurs and having His hair pulled out. Then, the scourging, where the flesh was ripped away as metal and glass imbedded strands of the Cat of Nine Tails drug across His back. All at the hands of unbelieving Roman soldiers. He was forced to perform the abasing act of staggering through the streets of the city, over whom he had wept, as condemned criminal. He willingly, I am certain, lay down and stretched out His arms to be nailed to the cross beam. When the crossbeam was raised into place, His naked body was exposed to endure the shame and ridicule by His countryman accorded a fellow Jew, nude in public. Only the most egregious crimes of the condemned caused the Romans to strip the condemned naked. All of this in front of His mother, family and friends. And then, the worst of the agonies, to be cursed by His Father, separated from Him and have the eternal life of His spirit extinguished as He stepped through the veil into Hell. To stop any of it, at any time, He had but utter one word, *help*. Angels, standing by would have sprung to His aide. It would have all been over for Him. To do so, however, would have doomed man for eternity, because man's redemption from sin, his hope for the justification of having sins expunged from his record forever and the glorious gift of being made acceptable, righteous in God's presence would never have been had Jesus said the word.

One of the words He did say was, "Father, forgive them for they do not know what they are doing." With these words Jesus classified the sin committed against Him, by any Jew or Roman involved in His death, under the Law of Unintentional Sin. I don't know that the Bible ever refers to this unintentional sin in such a way, but the whole of Leviticus Four deals with unintentional sin. All that was required to abate it was an offering by the priest. The High Priest

Chapter Six: The Garden of the Secret Place

was on the cross doing just that. Thus, no one was accounted as guilty of Jesus' death.

He exchanged His for ours. His scourging was an exchange for our healing. The crown of thorns, whose four inch thorns dug into His scalp, was the exchange for our peace of mind. Our sins, past, present and future became Him so that we might be made the righteousness of God. His dehydration was exchanged for our never having to be thirsty for knowledge of God. His defeat of Satan transferred authority over Darkness to us when His blood was accepted on the Heavenly Alter by the Father. Yes! By confessing Him as Lord (submitting our earthly life to His rule) and believing in the resurrection (establishing as truth that Jesus was not only the Son of God – a replication of God in the body of a man; that, indeed, He is alive now and forever) eternal life in God's presence is ours, now, not after we die. All of this is because of Jesus' atonement. It is upon this rock, Jesus Himself, that His church was built. [62]

If you have never truly given your life to Him, then now is the time and wherever you are is the place. Get on your knees, if you are able, and tell Him you are sorry that you have thought wrongly of Him (this is what repentance means). Acknowledge He is YOUR Lord now, while believing His resurrection is true. He is alive now and forever and has the desire and authority to grant your request for salvation. Write this date down and put it in your billfold or purse. And whenever you doubt your salvation, get it out and read it. And, remember. Then, as quickly as you can arrange it, confirm in the physical what happened in the spiritual by being baptized. It is the work of your faith this indeed happened. Any believer can baptize. It does not have to be done in a church.

Don't mistake what I am saying about the work of faith, please. None of us can do anything to be saved. It is the grace of God through faith, as I cited earlier. The hope of faith, confirmed in the natural realm by corresponding physical act, verifies in the spiritual realm our faith is alive and it will come to pass.

Somewhere back there we were talking about building houses. The most important finding was that our house of trust in God is built on the foundation of the atonement. This is the foundation you and I have which enables us to step into a place or situation that appears nothing at all like a promise of God. Or, when the Voice of God tells us is to do something, which at the time makes no common sense. When these kinds of situations confront us in life, how do we hear His voice? How do we learn to hear His voice in the hubbub of daily living?

I don't know if there is a formula for being able to hear God's voice. I do think the best and quickest way for a person to learn to

Chapter Six: The Garden of the Secret Place

---

hear from God is from another person's experience. So, if you don't mind and will indulge me, here is mine. I pray it will help you.

In Matthew 5, Jesus begins delivering the Sermon on the Mount with what are known as the Beatitudes. Beatitudes means a state of supreme happiness. The biblical number eight represents divine completion and rebirth. These eight are phases or steps toward Christian maturity. The fourth one says this: Blessed are those who hunger and thirst for righteousness, for they shall be satisfied. [63] I had gone through a period in which my pride was exposed to me. Through some really difficult days, God stripped it away from me, leaving me bereft of my self-esteem. My self-imagined importance and an unhealthy amount of self-righteousness were exposed to me. When He finished with me, it was a strange feeling.

I sensed emptiness, but it was not the kind of emptiness deep within that can't be filled until you allow God to fill it. This wasn't the emptiness of being without God and alone in the world. I was at peace, confidently aware God had been working in me, at my request, to purge out of me bad. Still there was an emptiness that began to demand to be filled. It was then I learned what the Bible means when it talks about being hungry and thirsty spiritually. It has been quite a few years ago, so the details are foggy, and I am not sure it works the same for everyone. The bottom line is this, I no longer was content with knowing about God; I wanted to know Him. I wanted to talk to Him and I wanted Him to talk back to me. I had questions; He had answers. He was wisdom; I needed wisdom. I wanted a relationship; not a religion. A couple of things happened. I do not remember which came first.

One was the understanding of what being made in the image of God meant. God was a speaking spirit and that is what I was. His words had the power to cause things that were not visible in this realm to be made visible. All by speaking words. The result, for me, was that anything I wanted to communicate with God needed to be through speech, not thoughts. Praying silently in my mind did not work for me anymore. Somewhat later, I realized I did not have to talk to God in a formal prayer, I could talk to Him just as you and I would.

About the same time, while reading the Book of James, the Holy Spirit pointed out to me a verse. I know it was the Holy Spirit, because the verse stood out so strongly. It was this: But if any of you lacks wisdom, let him ask of God, who gives to all generously and without reproach, and it will be given to him. But he must ask in faith without any doubting. [64] I grabbed onto that concept like a dog with a bone. It became mine. I had no doubt it would work. I remembered the last thing I had wondered about and asked God to explain

Chapter Six: The Garden of the Secret Place

it to me. Within two days, from something totally unrelated to the Bible or church stuff, the answer was right before me and I knew it was from God. I think the more educated among us would call that point cognitive recognition. Then, I started to ask God something and immediately be on the lookout for and expecting the answer. I do not think more than a week passed since that point in which I have not gotten my answer to whatever I asked on Him. It became the lamp that allowed me to find where His voice was located.

The Bible talks about the heart. I knew it wasn't talking about the organ, but I wasn't sure exactly what was meant. Out of my toolbox for aspiring Christians, I pulled out James 1:5 and asked. By then, I had learned that when I asked, if I would be quiet, the first thought that I would have would be the answer or a clue to the answer. The thought was a question. Where is the heart? My answer (out loud, by the way) was, in my chest. The next thought said to point to it. I did. Next, the thought was concentrate with your mind where it is in your chest. Then, move your thoughts to where your heart is located. It took a few days before I got the hang of it. Sure enough, I heard Him. It was that still, small voice I had heard others refer. I was so excited, I could barely contain myself. I had heard from God! Then, I later realized I could go to that place beforehand, or at the time, I asked God something.

Over time, I have learned to be very careful in the way I phrase my question to God. I ask only one question at a time. I think of what the answer would sound like to the question that I am thinking of asking. If I can't immediately envision an answer, I know to rephrase the question. If my thoughts seem cluttered, I tell (spoken words) my mind to shut down and receive no thoughts except those from God and then I ask the question again. There are times when I do not get an answer. Then, I will use another biblical way to hear from God. I mentioned this verse in the Introduction. Philippians 4: 6, 7 says this: Be anxious for nothing, but in everything by prayer and supplication with thanksgiving let your requests be made known to God. And the peace of God, which surpasses all comprehension, will guard your hearts and your minds in Christ Jesus. When the Bible says to do something, follow it to the letter. Here is the formula:

1. Be anxious for nothing — do not allow your mind to be worried about anything. Worry (anxiety) is a form of fear. Somebody has said that fear is False Evidence Appearing Real. I like that. Remember the lesson from our primary teacher in living the Christian life, James, Jesus' half-brother. Doubt (another form of the same) and faith can't occupy the same heart at the same time. God is a gentleman and He leaves, leaving you alone with doubt. When you have

Chapter Six: The Garden of the Secret Place

reached spiritual maturity, the way you get rid of doubt or anxiety is to tell it to go and instruct your mind what it is allowed to think.

2. Prayer and supplication with thanksgiving — Prayer means to talk to God. Supplication means to ask with urgency based on presumed need. Simple enough. When there is no emotion, it is impossible to have urgency. If you need it enough to bother the Creator of the universe with it, get passion behind it. When you have passion, expectation waits in the wings. Since you have the expectation at hand, thank Him for it. If you truly trust Him, he answered when you asked, anyway. He doesn't have to think about it. There is another example for us in the intensity God desires in supplication. When the twelve tribes were beginning to occupy the Land, they were told there would be certain cities set aside as Cities of Refuge.

Forty—eight cities, spread throughout the Land were allotted to the Levites who were Aaron's descendants. They would be the only ones to serve in the Temple as priests. Six of these forty—eight would also serve as a Cities of Refuge. If someone were to accidently kill a fellow Jew, he could flee to the City of Refuge to escape the wrath of the deceased's avengers. He would throw himself on the entrance to the home of an elder and pled his case for protection. If granted, he was required to live in the city until the current serving High Priest died. Now, you tell me the degree of sincerity in his plea for refuge. That is what biblical urgency is all about. Oh, by the way, our High Priest never dies.

3. God's peace will guard your heart and mind. God's peace acts as a gatekeeper for our spirits and minds. For example, if you ask God, should I accept this new job offer? Then, you have an undisturbed, relaxed spirit whenever you think about over the next few days; it is a green light from God to accept it. On the other hand, if thoughts about it cause you to be a little uncomfortable, disturbed, you are just not sure, God is saying not to take it. Peace will either leave Himself in place when the thought is entertained or step to the side just a bit to remove Himself.

Another way one may hear from God is what I call asking God for a mini—fleece. This idea comes from the story in Judges 6 about Gideon's anointing and commission to lead Israel against her enemies. Gideon is sure God has commissioned him to do this, but in the natural, what God is asking of him is overwhelming. To be certain of his commission, he asks God to confirm it with dew, on the ground under a fleece of wool. When God instructs you to take some kind of action and it is big enough in your life to cause you to be moved to the need for affirmation, I recommend this.

This is one of the rare times I recommend silent (thinking prayers). The reason is because you don't want the enemy to know what you are going to ask God to do. The principalities of darkness cannot read your mind; only suggest thoughts. Behind this veil of secrecy, ask God to show you something. Name what you want to see. Make it something you would not normally see, but not outside the realm of possibilities. Ask the Holy Spirit to make you aware when you see it. When you do see it, you will then have confirmation from God. One example would be to ask God to show you two birds normally not seen during the wintertime. Whatever it is, if God confirms, it will be within seven days.

Some may say this is unbelief. I would counter. God knows we are not good communicators in the spiritual realm. The motivation here is not one of, prove it was you, God; rather, please confirm what I think I heard from you, God, because I do not want to make a mistake. Not doing what God has told us can be just as bad as doing what He did not tell us. Paul tells us in Romans 15:4 that these stories we read in the Old Testament (the only scriptures available in his lifetime) are for our instruction. We are to learn from them.

As your walk of faith becomes steadier, the need for confirmations will become less rare. When you do need it, learn from Gideon, the hero. He was not looked back on by our icons of the faith as a faithless person.

Our search for the secret place of the Most High began with the fundamental necessity of the search; looking in the correct place. We began in the field of salvation. We dug in a plot which revealed the necessity of revamping our world view with that of God's through the transforming power of His words. Next to that plot was one whose yield to us was the hidden driving force of life; the God kind of love. Digging some more revealed the mechanism to function in this kind of environment which was biblical faith applied practically to one's life. As that digging was finished, we struck bedrock. The atonement of Jesus is the firm place upon which all of the soil rests. The only plot in which we had not dug was the one showing us how to communicate with God. Communication is two way. We found emotion and passion drove our words into His realm. We also found His words back to us could come in a variety of ways beneficial to us. All of these plots make up the garden of the secret place, but where is it?

We found it, but I am thinking we may not have stayed long enough for you to recognize it. The secret place is where I found the

Chapter Six: The Garden of the Secret Place

Spirit's still small voice inside my chest. It is where you can hear the Holy Spirit speak to you. When you first begin, you need to be alone and quiet. Speak out loud and tell your mind to receive no thoughts except those from God. It may be you need to speak to your mind more than once. Be firm, mean what you say. Concentrate and focus. You will hear His voice with your spiritual ears and understand the words in your consciousness. It is one of the most exhilarating experiences a Christian can have on the planet. I still get excited when I hear Him, but nothing like the first time. We have found it; the secret place of the Most High!

It is located in God's garden, a part of His kingdom, but not of this world. It is not buried separate from the other plots in which we dug, rather among them; just like Proverbs promised. He hid it for us to find and we found it. The Psalm, however, did not talk about finding the secret place. If you will remember, it talked about abiding, dwelling, living there.

This idea of dwelling is one of permanence. It is where you go when you *go home*. I don't mean just your house. When someone local asks where you live, you give them the address or the street or the area. When you are out of town, it is the city or, in my case, the large city of which my city is a suburb. It identifies where your life is lived. So, likewise, is the meaning in Psalm 91.

Living in the secret place means you have not only become practiced at being able to go to that spot in your chest whenever you want to, but practiced to the point you stay there most of the time, while living your life. It is what Paul meant when he said to walk by the Spirit in Galatians 5. [65] After presenting his great apologetic for the gospel he preached, explaining the purpose of the Law, explaining the power of Jesus' son ship and drawing the contrast between earthly inheritance and spiritual inheritance, he comes to the war between a flesh led life and spirit led life. I had been so focused on deeds of the flesh and fruit of the Spirit that I missed this revelation. I did not dwell on it, meditate about it and ask God to reveal what was hidden. In so doing, I passed right over one of the great mysteries in the New Testament; what walking by the Spirit means.

There are three benefits walking by the Spirit generates. They are:

1. You will not carry out the deeds of the flesh. [66] No more having to battle with sexual immorality, impurity, sensuality, idolatry, sorcery, enmities, strife, jealousy, outbursts of anger, disputes, dissensions, factions, envying, drunkenness, carousing, and things like these. [67] Don't read this, please, as my saying these urges are no longer present. They are, but

they have absolutely no power over you. They are dismissed as soon as you recognize them for who they are.

2. You are no longer under the Law. [68] Being under the Law means being under its jurisdiction. We all are under the jurisdiction of traffic laws issued by the proper governing authority wherever it is we drive. When we change jurisdictions, different traffic laws may apply. I understand that some states in the West have no speed limits on certain highways. There is no law on how fast you drive. That is exactly what it means to no longer be under God's Law. You are exempt from the requirements and resultant penalties. That is freedom! You do no longer have to will what to do; His Spirit is telling you what to do, so you naturally do the intent of the Law; without having to use self-discipline to keep it. I hope you see the difference. Your nature to act is in obedience; not to keep from being disobedient. One is produced by the Spirit; the other, by the will. The Old Testament is your friend; valuable instruction. Do not mentally throw it out or disregard it because Paul says you are no longer under the curse of the Law.

3. The fruit of the Spirit is produced in your life.[4] The fruit of a plant is produced as a result of its normal growth cycle. The

plant can't do anything to make the fruit form any quicker. In fact, the plant can't do anything other than grow. (Of course, this assumes all the conditions are proper.) So it is with us. The spiritual fruit we produce is just the natural response to the way we live our lives. Deeds of the flesh will always triumph in one not dwelling in the secret place. That is how to be sure you are still at home.

The Bible tells us in Genesis 2 that there was a garden east of Eden. Eden means pleasant. An easterly direction meant toward light, toward God's wisdom, knowledge and understanding. Knowing His ways and doing them would be a pleasant lifestyle. A garden, already planted and growing would only need tending, no labor was required to till. This garden, east of Eden, was the Kingdom of God on earth. Through the sacrifice of Jesus and the sanctifying work of the Holy Spirit in each of us, we can return there. The neighborhood isn't nice, like it was in the beginning, but it is still the best place on earth to live and raise a family.

CHAPTER SEVEN: SPIRITUAL WARFARE AND SUMMATION

Final thoughts

The last two chapters are not meant to be an exhaustive explanation on how to live life as a Christian. I have tried to outline important information everyone who calls themselves a Christian should know for the future ahead of us. One area I have not touched on is the influence of demonic activity in a person's life; what is written above assumes there is none.

The discussion of demons, by those who considers our society to be sophisticated, may want to relegate such a discussion to the ash heap of the absurd. If you are of this view, I would only ask you to consider why being sophisticated would have any effect on demonic activity when they were commonly accepted as being real during Jesus life. Paul clearly states that our struggle is not against flesh and blood, but against the rulers, against the powers, against the world forces of this darkness, against the spiritual *forces* of wickedness in the heavenly *places*.[5] So, why did I sidestep this information?

Demonic activity and spiritual warfare require greater depth of explanation than this book is designed to provide. To try and give basic information could do more harm to some readers than gain. Besides, there are others who are far more gifted in this area than me. One is my friend, Glynda Lomax Linkous. She has written several eBooks on the subject. No matter the resources to which you turn, I urge you to become well versed in the subject, with scriptural support, before you venture into this area. If you are not sure of what you are doing, you will be kicking the proverbial hornet's nest. I will only offer this suggestion: if things go consistently wrong in your life for no apparent reason or if you seem to have an unseen ceiling which keeps you from achieving your desires time and again, demonic activity *might* be the reason. Earnest prayer while fasting will give you direction. Just follow what I have said about the ways to hear from God and find solid teaching on the demonic.

A very uncertain, stressful and dangerous future is ahead of us. It will be like nothing Americans have ever experienced. Everyone will be affected. The *event* will happen during the time of the year after the blossom is gone and the formed grapes have begun to ripen, but before the harvest; the early summer months by astronomical

Chapter Seven: Spiritual Warfare and Summation

timing. Many Americans will die. I don't believe the entire country will experience the same level of the terror ahead, but the entire country will experience the results. There is no escape.

The repeating patterns of oppressing Israel to give up covenant land, with the corresponding natural disasters, are far beyond the possibility of coincidence. To deny that and offer some other explanation because it does not fit one's worldview is an affront to God's repeated cries of warning. Our national hubris that we have the strength and resolve to overcome, without acknowledging or mentioning God, is our forefather's council of admonitions come to roost. As I have watched our stiff-necked, international policies unfold in the Middle East, I cannot help but be reminded of the children's' stories the mythical Uncle Remus told about Ber' Rabbit and the Tar Baby. The harder the rabbit tried to get free, the more the tar ensnared him. So it is with the United States and the Middle East. That misguided policy and our ignorance of the Bible has put us in the crosshairs of God's judgment.

Isaiah's prophecy literally points directly to America. Though unnamed in Isaiah's time, it should now be clear to anyone seeking the truth of the Bible that Isaiah is not talking about Ethiopia. The unnamed nation is somewhere on the other side of Ethiopia. We cannot run and we cannot hide. We are going to take a whipping.

I first thought God description to Isaiah was nuclear event(s). The idea of dazzling light and a cloud of nuclear fallout certainly satisfies what God said, except even several would not cover the whole of America. A collapsed economy and nuclear attacks would certainly leave us vulnerable to terrorists and invasions but how could the world be alerted and be watching? Whatever *it* is, America will never be the same.

The best hope is to dwell in the secret place of the Most High and trust Him to be your fortress. I am confident the Holy Spirit won't be telling everyone the same thing. It will depend on where one lives. My counsel to you is to get to the secret place as quickly as you can and move in.

Death seems horrible to us. God sees death, not as the end, but as the beginning of another cycle of life. That new cycle may be horrible; it may be glorious. Whichever it will be is determined now, in this life. We don't get to choose then; we have to choose now. If you are not certain you have chosen Jesus, my advice would be to choose Him now. My experience has been that He is a much better deal. I have tried both. For the Christian, after the end of this cycle of living – this human life — everything in will be good. And if it is not good, it is not yet the end.

APPENDIX A

Isaiah 18 rendered in various translations

The Net Bible

The land of buzzing wings is as good as dead, the one beyond the rivers of Cush,

^{18:2} that sends messengers by sea, who glide over the water's surface in boats made of papyrus. Go, you swift messengers, to a nation of tall, smooth—skinned people, to a people that are feared far and wide, to a nation strong and victorious, whose land rivers divide.

^{18:3} All you who live in the world, who reside on the earth, you will see a signal flag raised on the mountains; you will hear a trumpet being blown.

^{18:4} For this is what the Lord has told me: "I will wait and watch from my place, like scorching heat produced by the sunlight, like a cloud of mist in the heat of harvest."

¹⁸:⁵ For before the harvest, when the bud has sprouted, and the ripening fruit appears, he will cut off the unproductive shoots with pruning knives; he will prune the tendrils.

¹⁸:⁶ They will all be left for the birds of the hills and the wild animals; the birds will eat them during the summer, and all the wild animals will eat them during the winter.

¹⁸:⁷ At that time tribute will be brought to the LORD who commands armies, by a people that are tall and smooth-skinned, a people that are feared far and wide, a nation strong and victorious, whose land rivers divide. The tribute will be brought to the place where the LORD who commands armies has chosen to reside, on Mount Zion. [69]

New International Version

Woe to the land of whirring wings along the rivers of Cush,[6] which sends envoys by sea in papyrus boats over the water. Go, swift messengers, to a people tall and smooth-skinned, to a people feared far and wide, an aggressive nation of strange speech, whose land is divided by rivers.

³All you people of the world, you who live on the earth, when a banner is raised on the mountains, you will see it, and when a trumpet sounds, you will hear it.

⁴This is what the LORD says to me: "I will remain quiet and will look on from my dwelling place,

like shimmering heat in the sunshine, like a cloud of dew in the heat of harvest."

⁵For, before the harvest, when the blossom is gone and the flower becomes a ripening grape, he will cut off the shoots with pruning knives, and cut down and take away the spreading branches.

⁶They will all be left to the mountain birds of prey and to the wild animals; the birds will feed on them all summer, the wild animals all winter.

⁷At that time gifts will be brought to the LORD Almighty from a people tall and smooth-skinned, from a people feared far and wide, an aggressive nation of strange speech, whose land is divided by rivers—the gifts will be brought to Mount Zion, the place of the Name of the LORD Almighty. ⁷⁰

The King James Version

18Woe to the land shadowing with wings, Which *is* beyond the rivers of Ethiopia:

²That sendeth ambassadors by the sea, Even in vessels of bulrushes upon the waters, *saying*, Go, ye swift messengers, To a nation scattered and peeled, To a people terrible from their beginning hitherto; A nation meted out and trodden down, Whose land the rivers have spoiled!

³All ye inhabitants of the world, and dwellers on the earth, See ye, when he lifteth up an ensign on the mountains; And when he bloweth a trumpet, hear ye.

⁴For so the LORD said unto me, I will take my rest, and I will consider in my dwelling place like a clear heat upon herbs, *And* like a cloud of dew in the heat of harvest.

⁵For afore the harvest, when the bud is perfect, and the sour grape is ripening in the flower, He shall both cut off the sprigs with pruning hooks, and take away *and* cut down the branches.

⁶They shall be left together unto the fowls of the mountains, and to the beasts of the earth: and the fowls shall summer upon them, and all the beasts of the earth shall winter upon them.

⁷In that time shall the present be brought unto the LORD of hosts of a people scattered and peeled, and from a people terrible from their beginning hitherto; a nation meted out and trodden under foot, whose land the rivers have spoiled, to the place of the name of the LORD of hosts, the mount Zion. [71]

The Holman Christian Standard Bible

Ah! The land of buzzing insect wings beyond the rivers of Cush[7] sends couriers by sea, in reed vessels the waters. Go, swift messengers, to a nation tall and smooth—skinned, to a people feared far and near, a powerful nation with a strange language, whose land is divided by rivers.

³ All you inhabitants of the world and you who live on the earth, when a banner is raised on the mountains, look! When a trumpet sounds, listen!

⁴ For, the LORD said to me: I will quietly look out from My place, like shimmering heat in sunshine, like a rain cloud in harvest heat.

⁵ For before the harvest, when the blossoming is over and the blossom becomes a ripening grape, He will cut off the shoots with a pruning knife, and tear away and remove the branches.

⁶ They will all be left for the birds of prey on the hills and for the wild animals of the land. The birds will spend the summer on them, and all the animals, the winter on them.

⁷ At that time a gift will be brought to Yahweh of Hosts from a people tall and smooth-skinned, a people feared far and near, a powerful nation with a strange language, whose land is divided by rivers—to Mount Zion, the place of the name of Yahweh of Hosts. [72]

The Good News Translation

Beyond the rivers of Ethiopia there is a land where the sound of wings is heard. From that land ambassadors come down the Nile in boats made of reeds. Go back home, swift messengers! Take a message back to your land divided by rivers, to your strong and powerful nation, to your tall and smooth-skinned people, who are feared all over the world.

3 Listen, everyone who lives on earth! Look for a signal flag to be raised on the tops of the mountains! Listen for the blowing of the bugle! The LORD said to me, "I will look down from heaven as quietly as the dew forms in the warm nights of harvest time, as serenely as the sun shines in the heat of the day. Before the grapes are gathered, when the blossoms have all fallen and the grapes are ripening, the enemy will destroy the Ethiopians as easily as a knife cuts branches from a vine. The corpses of their soldiers will be left exposed to the birds and the wild animals. In summer the birds will feed on them, and in winter, the animals."

7 A time is coming when the LORD Almighty will receive offerings from this land divided by rivers, this strong and powerful nation, this tall and smooth—skinned people, who are feared all over the world. They will come to Mount Zion, where the LORD Almighty is worshipped. [73]

The English Standard Version

Ah, land of whirring wings that is beyond the rivers of Cush, ²which sends ambassadors by the sea, in vessels of papyrus on the waters! Go, you swift messengers, to a nation tall and smooth, to a people feared near and far, a nation mighty and conquering, whose land the rivers divide.

³All you inhabitants of the world, you who dwell on the earth, when a signal is raised on the mountains, look! When a trumpet is blown, hear!

⁴For thus the LORD said to me: "I will quietly look from my dwelling like clear heat in sunshine, like a cloud of dew in the heat of harvest."

⁵For before the harvest, when the blossom is over, and the flower becomes a ripening grape,

he cuts off the shoots with pruning hooks, and the spreading branches he lops off and clears away.

⁶They shall all of them be left to the birds of prey of the mountains and to the beasts of the earth. And the birds of prey will summer on them, and all the beasts of the earth will winter on them.

⁷At that time tribute will be brought to the LORD of hosts from a people tall and smooth, from a people feared near and far, a nation mighty and conquering, whose land the rivers divide, to Mount Zion, the place of the name of the LORD of hosts. [74]

APPENDIX B

Christian foreshadowing in the Jewish wedding

The Jewish wedding was a major event for the Jewish community. The betrothal and ceremony of the First Century was different from ours. The ceremony's celebration lasted seven days. The significance of the number seven in scripture is that it represents completion; things have been summed up. The time from betrothal to ceremony usually took about a year.

About a year earlier than the actual ceremony, the bridegroom to be would come to the home of his proposed bride. In his best clothes, he would come bearing three things; wine, a glass and a document. Of the three, the document was the centerpiece of the betrothal. The document is known as the *ketubah*. In Hebrew it means *that which is written*. The ketubah accomplishes many things. These are:

- It is a contract signed by both bride and groom and thereby an enforceable, legal document between the parties.

- It includes the price paid for the bride. The bride was her father's property and this amounted to the purchase price for her.
- It contains the promises that the groom must keep and the rights to which the bride is entitled.
- It is the unalienable (can never be sold, traded or transferred) right of the bride. It promised that the groom would work for her, honor her, support her and maintain her in truth, but most importantly, that he would never leave her side all the days of her life.

The bride, however, had a say in the matter of the marriage proposal. The ketubah was formally agreed to with a glass of wine. The groom would take a sip and set the glass in front of the bride. If she drank from it, she signaled her acceptance. If she did not, both her father and the groom would be humiliated with her rejection. Thus, she was under pressure. If she accepted, the *ketubah* would then be signed by bride and bridegroom and witnessed by two outside the family. The couple were then considered married, though the marriage had not yet been consummated. A formal divorce decree, a *Get,* would have to be granted to dissolve the marriage and annul the ketubah.

Appendix B

The groom would then retire to his father's home to make preparations for his new bride and earn funds to satisfy his financial commitment under the ketubah. This period was known as the betrothal. (It was during this period Gabriel visited Mary.) The couple would see each other during the betrothal, under the eye of a chaperone. When the bridegroom's father said all was ready, from one to four years in the First Century, the groom would go back to the bride's father's home to get the bride.

During the betrothal the bridegroom's father was making financial arrangements to host the event. When he was ready financially, he would appoint a headwaiter, head steward or master of the banquet. His title varies, but usually, it was a trusted friend. His responsibility was to see to all the details of the wedding celebration, leaving the father free to visit with his guests. Now, here is the first element in the foreshadowing; each of us who know the Lord, have been given a ketubah — it's the Bible. It lays out what God will do for us in this life and beyond. The purchase price for us is, of course, Jesus' crucifixion. Our consent to accept it as the true guide for our life is to accept the blood sacrifice of Jesus as the substitute for our own. We are de facto then, the bride of Christ.

The Jewish wedding was all about the groom's father.
- He approved to whom the proposal would be made.

- He directed the composition of the document.
- He received the purchase price.
- He was not present at the proposal.
- He determined where the bride would live in his house.
- He invited the guests and made the preparations.
- He said when the preparations were complete and approved the groom to bring her to their home for the ceremony.
- He appointed a Head Steward to supervise the procedures.

Once the betrothal period was declared over, the ceremony could take place. Remember, these two were already married. The ceremony was the physical consummation of the marriage and it too, had its traditions. The bridegroom and his friends would come to the bride's home. Almost always this happened at night. They would come from the bridegroom's home via torchlight and with much gaiety, timed to arrive at the bride's home at midnight. (The symbolism of midnight is the midpoint of darkness, a clue to the timing of the rapture in relation to the tribulation.) Imagine sitting on a hill and witnessing this group traverse below you. Torches would be lighting their way and the ground around them. There would be much laughing, the intermittent blowing of the shofars and jocular conversation. Gaiety would have been captured in time.

Jesus alludes to this in His comforting discourse to the disciples (and by extension — believers) in John 14:2-8. I want to quote this comforting verse again from another translation. He says, "In My Father's house is many dwelling places; if not, I would have told you. I am going away to prepare a place for you. If I go away and prepare a place for you, I will come back and receive you to Myself, so that where I am you may be also."[8] [Another aside: The words *dwelling places* (translated as *mansions* in the King James) are thought by some as being fancy homes. The original text would differ. Dwelling places is from the Greek word *mone*. It has the idea of living together. So, the idea is not living in a physical place; rather, being a part of God's family or His house.]

On the night the bridegroom's father says, the guests gather at the father's home while the groom and his entourage, including one known as the friend of the bridegroom, have started their journey. The bride knows this day is approaching. She begins setting candles in her window each evening, then bathing and putting on her wedding dress in order to be ready on the big night. (The analogy here is the lives of Believer's produce fruit which give light in the dark world to unbeliever's, we are washed clean with the Word of God and thereby, wear the gown of salvation and the robe of righteousness.) Friends of the bride, the bridesmaids, are waiting outside of her home for the groom with hand lamps to light the way for him. (I'll cover this symbolism later.) The friend of the bridegroom loudly announces their arrival and all go in the bride's home. The bride and groom then retire to a room, known as the *Chuppah*, for that night alone. There the wedding is consummated, while witnesses wait outside the door. The friend of the bridegroom listens for the bridegroom's announcement that the marriage has been consummated and then, he announces it to the joy of the witnesses. If this is not enough for Twenty-first Century propriety, this next event probably will be.

The room's identity, the Chuppah, comes from a square cloth placed on the wedding bed in anticipation of the couple's arrival. It will retain the stains of the virgin bride's blood and bodily fluids released during the consummation. When the couple emerges from the room, the groom will present the stained Chuppah to witnesses chosen by the bride's parents to confirm her virginity and the consummation. It will later be returned to the bride. It is her proof should she ever be accused of not being a virgin on this night; read, grounds for divorce.

In the midst of other stories explaining the Kingdom of Heaven at the end of the age, Jesus singles out a story about a bridegroom's party arriving at a bride's house in Matthew 21. Jesus says, "Then the kingdom of heaven will be like ten virgins who took their lamps and went out to meet the bridegroom. Five of them were foolish and five were wise. For when the foolish took their lamps, they took no oil with them, but the wise took flasks of oil with their lamps. As the bridegroom was delayed, they all became drowsy and slept. But at midnight there was a cry, 'Here is the bridegroom! Come out to meet him.' Then all those virgins arose and trimmed their lamps. And the foolish said to the wise, 'Give us some of your oil, for our lamps are going out.' But the wise answered, saying, 'since there will not be enough for us and for you, go rather to the dealers and buy for yourselves.' And while they were going to buy, the bridegroom came, and those who were ready went in with him to the marriage feast, and the door was shut. Afterward the other virgins came also, saying, 'Lord, lord, open to us.' But he answered, 'Truly, I say to you, I do not know you.' Watch therefore, for you know neither the day nor the hour." [9]

This is the symbolism, or foreshadowing, I would like to share from this Parable of the Ten Virgins.

- This event takes place in darkness, only a few hours into the new day which, remember. Begins at sunset. Days are counted by God from evening to evening. We are told in 2 Peter 3:8, in connection with the Day of the Lord (the Tribulation), that with the Lord one day is like one thousand years and a thousand years like one day. So, the one thousand years of the Millennium Kingdom will begin in spiritual darkness, just as the earth in Genesis 1:1. One cycle ends; another, begins. Spiritual darkness and chaos will be the general condition of the world. Halfway through this spiritual darkness (tribulation) the rapture will occur.

- Oil, fresh oil, is the fuel for the light of the lamp. The imagery here is what the menorah represents. A candle stand of solid gold with branches for seven candles known in Hebrew as a menorah stood in the Holy Place on the north wall. What the menorah did physically was provide light for the priests who entered. In the spiritual sense, the menorah's light is God's wisdom, understanding and knowledge He chooses to reveal to man. Placed on the north wall, from where enemy attacks come, illuminate God's wisdom for protection against their attacks.

- I must confess I struggled with who these bridesmaids represent. Maybe you already know and I am just catching up. For everybody else, here is what I understand Jesus to be saying. Remember, He is talking about the Kingdom of God at the end of the Age. The bride represents the church. Her friends are the ones who provide her light and are presumed to be her friends. They function as menorah to the body of Christ: teachers revealing God, if you will. Sleepy virgins who are low on oil represent those teachers who mix their teaching with a combination of truth and falsehood. Peter warns of these in Chapter Three. His implication is that they lead the unwitting away from a spotless and blameless lifestyle, through the distortion of scripture. These are the false teachers of 2 Peter 2:1. They are the ones Jesus singles out in Matthew 7:22, 23 at the end of the Sermon on the Mount. He says that many will say to Him in that day (Day of the Lord), "Lord, Lord, did we not prophesy in Your name, and in Your name cast out demons and in Your name perform many works of power? And then I will declare to them, 'I never knew you. Depart from Me, you who practice lawlessness." Almost the same words are used here by Jesus. They have no relationship with Him. They know about Him, but eminently know Him. When the Bible mentions fools or the foolish it means those who do not follow God's instructions for living. Notice, they were shut out because they had no relationship. Relationship with God can only exist in righteousness, which is doing things God's way. At the most crucial time of their ministry, they had to get the truth of the gospel from outside of themselves. They were not deemed creditable witnesses and were thus, shut out forever.

- Jesus closes with the admonition to be on the alert. Be on the alert for what is a fair question. It is connected to the next phrase for you know neither the day nor the hour. It does not mean that we can't know when this is going to take place, as many falsely think. This is a Jewish idiom for the first of the fall feats, what most of us know as Rosh Hashanah. Rosh Hashanah means head of the year; the first day of the civil year. It is the first day of the month of Tishri, the seventh month of the religious year. The religious year begins on the first day of the month of Nisan, in the spring. Rosh Hashanah is properly known as the Feast of Teruah (blasting), also known as the Feast of Trumpets. So, what Jesus is saying is that the acting out of this parable in real life (the arrival of the bridegroom to claim his bride from her earthly father's house) will take place on a future Feast of Trumpets. We know this event as the rapture. We are warned to be alert because there will be signs alerting those who are alive at the time.

The wedding ceremony of today continues to have symbolism for the Christian. The bridegroom represents Jesus; the bride represents the Church. The bride being given away represents the rapture. The ring represents eternity, without beginning or end. Taking her husband's name represents the inheritance promised by the Father of spending eternity with Him. The Wedding Night represents joining into the Oneness with Jesus, our eternal state. The ceremony is a rehearsal for the rapture. The whole of the wedding celebration, ceremony and reception, is the Marriage Supper of the Lamb. There is a reason we celebrate at weddings.

END NOTES

Chapter One: Storms

[1] Junger, Sebastian (2000). *The Perfect Storm*. New York: W. W. Norton & Company.

[2] The Perfect Storm. Dir. Wolfgang Petersen. Perf. George Clooney, Mark Wahlberg, Diane Lane. Warner Bros. 2000.

[3] Article, Middle East Policy Council (http://www.mepc.org/journal/middle-east-policy-archives/friend-re-evaluating-bush-and-israel)

[4] *The Harbinger: The Ancient Mystery that Holds the Secret of America's Future.* 2012. (272) Frontline.

[5] George Escobar. Dir. *The Isaiah 9:10 Judgment: Is There an Ancient Mystery that Foretells America's Future?* Jonathan Cahn. WND, 2012. DVD.

Chapter Two: Disasters

[6] Koenig, William R. & McTernenan, John P. (1991) *Israel: The Blessing or the Curse.* (200) Oklahoma City, OK: Hearthstone Publishers, Ltd.

[7] William R. Koenig, *Eye To Eye: Facing The Consequences of Dividing Israel.* About Him. 2008

[8] John P. McTernan, As *America Has Done to Israel.* Xulon Press. 2006.

[9] Mendenhall, G. E., & Herion, G. A. (1992). Covenant. In D. N. Freedman (Ed.). *Vol. 1: The Anchor Yale Bible Dictionary* (D. N. Freedman, Ed.) (1180). New York: Doubleday.

[10] Wilkerson, Bruce. *Prayer of Jabez: Breaking Through to the Blessed Life.* Multnomah Publishers 2000.

[11] 1 Chronicles 4:9

[12] *New American Standard Bible: 1995 update.* 1995 (Ge 12:3). LaHabra, CA: The Lockman Foundation.

[3] http://www.whitehouse.gov/the-press-office/press-conference-president-trinidad-and-tobago-4192009

[14] http://www.huffingtonpost.com/2009/06/19/us-joins-un-human-rights_n_217932.html

[15] http://liveshots.blogs.foxnews.com/2010/04/19/obama-and-israel-showdown-at-the-un/

[16] Wikipedia Online Encyclopedia, (http://en.wikipedia.org/wiki/Deepwater_Horizon_oil_spill

[17] http://www.csmonitor.com/World/Backchannels/2011/0520/What-s-so-shocking-about-Obama-mentioning-1967-borders

[18] http://freebeacon.com/u-n-human-rights-council-calls-for-boycott-of-u-s-companies/

[19] *New American Standard Bible: 1995 update.* 1995 (James 4: 8). LaHabra, CA: The Lockman Foundation.

[20] Robert H. Bork. *Slouching Toward Gomorra: Modern Liberalism and the American Decline.* Harper Collins. 1996.

CHAPTER THREE: THE UNNAMED NATION

[21] *New American Standard Bible: 1995 update.* 1995 (Pr 25:2). LaHabra, CA: The Lockman Foundation.

[22] *New American Standard Bible: 1995 update.* 1995 (Mt 13:44). LaHabra, CA: The Lockman Foundation.

[23] From *The Apocrypha and Pseudepigrapha of the Old Testament* by R.H. Charles, Oxford: Clarendon Press, 1913
Scanned and edited by Joshua Williams, Northwest Nazarene College, 1995

[24] http://en.wikipedia.org/wiki/Lives_of_the_Prophets

End Notes

[25] Clements, R. E. (1992). Woe. In D. N. Freedman (Ed.), . *Vol. 6: The Anchor Yale Bible Dictionary* (D. N. Freedman, Ed.) (945). New York: Doubleday.

[26] *New American Standard Bible: 1995 update*. 1995 (Is 66:8). LaHabra, CA: The Lockman Foundation.

[27] *New American Standard Bible: 1995 update*. 1995 (Eze 4:4–6). LaHabra, CA: The Lockman Foundation.

[28] http://www.alphanewsdaily.com/mathprophecy2.html

[29] *New American Standard Bible: 1995 update*. 1995 (Is 18:1). LaHabra, CA: The Lockman Foundation.

[30] www.thehronicleproject.org, a research group who has discovered the self-defining Hebrew alphabet characters giving more clear insight into the meaning of words in the bible.

[31] *New American Standard Bible: 1995 update*. 1995 (Is 18:2). LaHabra, CA: The Lockman Foundation.

CHAPTER FOUR: THE BAD NEWS

[32] *New American Standard Bible: 1995 update*. 1995 (Is 18:3). LaHabra, CA: The Lockman Foundation.

[33] *New American Standard Bible: 1995 update*. 1995 (Is 18:4). LaHabra, CA: The Lockman Foundation.

[34] *New American Standard Bible: 1995 update*. 1995 (1 John 1:5). LaHabra, CA: The Lockman Foundation.

[35] *New American Standard Bible: 1995 update*. 1995 (Genesis 1:2). LaHabra, CA: The Lockman Foundation.

[36] *New American Standard Bible: 1995 update*. 1995 (Is 18:5). LaHabra, CA: The Lockman Foundation.

[37] Bruce Wilkinson, David Kopp. *The Secrets of the Vine*. 2006. Colorado Springs, Co. Waterbook Multnomah Publishing Group.

[38] *New American Standard Bible: 1995 update*. 1995 (Ge 1:14–15). LaHabra, CA: The Lockman Foundation.

[39] http://www2.jpl.nasa.gov/sl9/

[40] F. Michael Maloof. *A Nation Forsaken, EMP: The Escalating Threat of an American Catastrophe.* 2013. WND Books

[41] *New American Standard Bible: 1995 update.* 1995 (Is 18:6). LaHabra, CA: The Lockman Foundation.

[42] *New American Standard Bible: 1995 update.* 1995 (Is 18:7). LaHabra, CA: The Lockman Foundation.

CHAPTER FIVE: THE NARROW WAY

[43] *New American Standard Bible: 1995 update.* 1995 (Eph 4:13). LaHabra, CA: The Lockman Foundation.

[44] *New American Standard Bible: 1995 update.* 1995 (Col 1:27). LaHabra, CA: The Lockman Foundation.

[45] *New American Standard Bible: 1995 update.* 1995 (Lk 4:18–19). LaHabra, CA: The Lockman Foundation. Author's note: whenever an Old Testament scripture is quoted in the New Testament, the words are capitalized.

[46] *New American Standard Bible: 1995 update.* 1995 (Eph 6:12). LaHabra, CA: The Lockman Foundation.

[47] Arndt, W., Danker, F. W., & Bauer, W. (2000). *A Greek-English lexicon of the New Testament and other early Christian literature* (3rd ed.) (199). Chicago: University of Chicago Press.

[48] *New American Standard Bible: 1995 update.* 1995 (1 Jn 2:14). LaHabra, CA: The Lockman Foundation.

[49] *New American Standard Bible: 1995 update.* 1995 (1 Jn 2:16). LaHabra, CA: The Lockman Foundation.

[50] *New American Standard Bible: 1995 update.* 1995 (Mk 11:24). LaHabra, CA: The Lockman Foundation.

[51] *New American Standard Bible: 1995 update.* 1995 (Php 4:6). LaHabra, CA: The Lockman Foundation.

[52] *New American Standard Bible: 1995 update.* 1995 (Rom 8:29). LaHabra, CA: The Lockman Foundation.

End Notes

[53] The Most Exotic Marigold Hotel. Dir. John Madden. Perf. Judy Dench, Tom Wilkinson, Bill Nighly. Movie. Fox Searchlight Pictures. 2012.

[54] *New American Standard Bible: 1995 update.* 1995 (1 John 5:21). LaHabra, CA: The Lockman Foundation

[55] Louw, J. P., & Nida, E. A. (1996). *Vol. 1: Greek-English lexicon of the New Testament: Based on semantic domains* (electronic ed. of the 2nd edition.) (539). New York: United Bible Societies.

[56] *New American Standard Bible: 1995 update.* 1995 (Heb 12:5–6). LaHabra, CA: The Lockman Foundation.

[57] *New American Standard Bible: 1995 update.* 1995 (Php 4:7). LaHabra, CA: The Lockman Foundation.

CHAPTER SIX: THE GARDEN OF THE SECRET PLACE

[58] *The New King James Version.* 1982 (Ps 91:1). Nashville: Thomas Nelson.

[59] Matthew 6:10.

[60] *New American Standard Bible: 1995 update.* 1995 (Lk 6:45–46). LaHabra, CA: The Lockman Foundation.

[61] *New American Standard Bible: 1995 update.* 1995 (James 1:6-8). LaHabra, CA: The Lockman Foundation.

[62] Matthew 16:18 is where Jesus gives the name Peter to Simeon. Peter (petros) means stone, small in size. Jesus goes on to say that upon this rock (petra), which means large stone, He will build His church. The church is built on Jesus, not Peter.

[63] *New American Standard Bible: 1995 update.* 1995 (Mt 5:6). LaHabra, CA: The Lockman Foundation.

[64] *New American Standard Bible: 1995 update.* 1995 (Jas 1:5–6). LaHabra, CA: The Lockman Foundation.

[65] *New American Standard Bible: 1995 update.* 1995 (Ga 5:19–21). LaHabra, CA: The Lockman Foundation.

[66] *New American Standard Bible: 1995 update.* 1995 (Gal 5: 18). LaHabra, CA: The Lockman Foundation.

[67] *New American Standard Bible: 1995 update.* 1995 (Gal 5: 25). LaHabra, CA: The Lockman Foundation.

[68] *New American Standard Bible: 1995 update.* 1995 (Eph 6:12). LaHabra, CA: The Lockman Foundation.

APPENDIX A

[69] Biblical Studies Press. (2006). *The NET Bible First Edition; Bible. English. NET Bible.; The NET Bible* (Is 18:1–7). Biblical Studies Press.

[70] *The Holy Bible: New International Version.* 1996 (electronic ed.) (Is 18:1–7). Grand Rapids, MI: Zondervan.

[71] *The Holy Bible: King James Version.* 2009 (Electronic Edition of the 1900 Authorized Version.) (Is 18). Bellingham, WA: Logos Research Systems, Inc.

[72] *The Holy Bible: Holman Christian standard version.* 2009 (Is 18:1–7). Nashville: Holman Bible Publishers.

[73] American Bible Society. (1992). *The Holy Bible: The Good news Translation* (2nd ed.) (Is 18:1–7). New York: American Bible Society.

[74] *The Holy Bible: English Standard Version.* 2001 (Is 18:1–7). Wheaton: Standard Bible Society.